CYBER-COUNSELING
FOR MUSLIM CLIENTS

A Muslim psychologist addressing
psychospiritual problems faced by Muslims

CYBER-COUNSELING

FOR MUSLIM CLIENTS

MALIK BADRI

The Other Press
Kuala Lumpur

Published by
The Other Press Sdn. Bhd.
607 Mutiara Majestic
Jalan Othman
46000 Petaling Jaya
Selangor, Malaysia
www.ibtbooks.com

The Other Press is affiliated with Islamic Book Trust.

Perpustakaan Negara Malaysia   Cataloguing-in-Publication Data

Malik Badri
        Cyber-Counseling for Muslim Clients / Malik B. Badri.
        ISBN 978-967-0957-02-9
        1. Counseling psychology--Technological innovations.
        2. Counseling psychology--Miscellanea.
        3. Islam--Psychology. I. Title.
        616.891402854678

To Babiker Badri,
his son Yousif and his grandson Gasim

Contents

Preface

One late night in 1995, my old table telephone rang. I was then professor in the International Institute of Islamic Thought and Civilization (ISTAC) in Kuala Lumpur, Malaysia. At that time, when the telephone in my flat rang at a very late hour, I used to excitedly pick it up fearing that I might get bad news from my far away home in Sudan. However, unexpectedly and pleasantly, it was from my dear brilliant student and friend, a gifted Yemini American, Omer Awass. In his character, Omer combined the romanticism of the Yemini Arab with the rationality, creativity and pragmatism of the American. He is endowed with superior intellect and a tremendous capacity for deductive reasoning. As a student, his original thoughts were often much higher than those of his classmates. I often felt that he had been bored. He called me to ask for my help in establishing a cyber-counseling program for the famous Islam-online site. He discovered that many of the questions that were posed by the viewers to the clerics were actually psycho-spiritual in nature and that a Muslim psychologist can be of more help to them. He wanted me to initiate with him such a useful forum. I readily accepted.

After we started the cyber-counseling program, I discovered that Omer has another great gift. He was exceptionally fast in typing. He quickly typed the question that was being dictated to him by phone. He read it to me and then typed my answer in the same fast way. He then put it in the internet and sent it to the one who asked the question. Every week, for over six months, I used to hold the telephone, answering questions, counseling and advising for more than one and a half hours. The collected questions and the solutions of problems given in my responses form the basis of the book I am now presenting. As the reader will find, the issues discussed were quite varied and they came from different parts of the world. The questions and answers in the book a variety of issues and problems that affect Muslims in this changing world of globalization. Though most issues dealt with problems arising from marital disharmony and conflicts in dysfunctional families, and anxiety and mood disorders, the forum received interesting questions about various issues in psychology such as parapsychology, drug addiction and the influence of the mind over the body. I selected 44 questions for this book.

Some of the young troubled persons got hold of my email. I was happy to hear from them that my answers were helpful to them, but they often brought up new issues that I had to answer. I included their questions and my answers to them in the book though they did not come through the regular cyber-counseling forum. In preparing the manuscript for publication, I only edited some of the questions and my answers to them and added a few more ideas; but I did my best to preserve the spontaneous extemporaneous approach that I followed. So the book does not rigidly adhere to scholarly referencing format of footnotes and bibliographical entries. Rather, it is simply a collection of my spontaneous answers to questions posed by Muslims in my cyber-counseling sessions. I tried to provide them with solutions to their problems from an Islamic perspective. My answers to these questions are based on my counseling methodology of giving an Islamic modeled therapy to troubled Muslims. I hope that some of the answers will continue to help other readers who have similar questions or who suffer from similar problems. As expected, the senders of the questions signed anonymously, but the few of them who wrote their real names did not object to their problem being exposed in the Internet.

All the material of the book remained saved in my laptop and desk top computers for more than twenty years. It is only after I was offered the prestigious Chair of Ibn Khaldun in the International Islamic University that I could find available time to turn the collected material into a book. At this juncture, I would like to express my profound gratitude to the Rector of the International Islamic University Malaysia and the University Senate for approving my appointment to the Chair of Ibn Khaldun. I am also grateful to the Dean of the Kulliyyah of Revealed Knowledge and Human Sciences who set up the Chair. I also gratefully acknowledge the support of Professor Gasim, the President of the Ahfad University for approving my appointment. Finally, I would like to thank Dr. Omer Awass who was the real initiator of the whole project and to Dr. Umar Abdurahman for editing the book.

Malik B. Badri
Kuala Lumpur, June 1st, 2015

Foreword

I had the pleasure of meeting Dr. Malik Badri nearly 20 years ago in the fall of 1995. At that time I was a graduate student at the then International Institute of Islamic Thought and Civilization (ISTAC) in Malaysia where Dr. Badri was a professor and taught courses on Islam and psychology. I had the privilege of taking his course on the medical treatise of 9th century physician Abu Zaid al-Balkhi, whose study cases on psychological treatments have now been translated from Arabic to English by Dr. Badri under the title, *Sustenance of the Soul*. Yet many may find this mixture of Islamic religious elements and sociological and scientific discipline like psychology to be strange. However, the pertinent question to be asked is whether social sciences are independent from religious worldviews and cultural forms?

This question is best answered in another earlier work of Dr. Badri entitled *The Dilemma of Muslim Psychologists*. In this work, he critically examined the damage caused by Western trained Muslim psychologists in their application of Western oriented psychological theories, especially Freudian psychoanalysis, to the larger Muslim public. Dr. Badri strongly argued against such applications as many of these theories were reflections of Western societies and their particular historical reality rather than representations of any 'objective' science. These theories might not be valid after all. Treating patients from other cultural backgrounds using such theories would exacerbate rather than solve their psychological problems. Essentially, Dr. Badri recognized that many theories in the social sciences, especially psychology, were not independent from the historical and cultural contexts in which they developed because essentially, they were just offshoots. Hence, there is a need to develop psychological theoretical studies and practices from an Islamic perspective that would address peculiar issues that were not addressed by Western-based psychological theories.

This brings me to the subject matter of this book. It was with this understanding that in early 2002, I reached out to Dr. Badri to assist me in initiating cyber counseling session guide for a new job I began with Islam Online shortly after my return to the United States from my lengthy study sojourn abroad. As my work entailed that I host online forums that would address the social, religious, and political concerns of the websites predominately Muslim audience, I began to notice that some of the issues raised in these forums were of an emotional nature, which could not be addressed by our guests on these forums. The only one I can think of who could competently address some of these concerns was Dr. Badri; hence, I contacted him. Dr. Badri who was still in Malaysia, proposed we hold an online Islamic counseling forum that would give counseling sessions to those who needed them. He graciously agreed to participate as a counselor and we started to hold this online forum on a weekly basis for a period over six months, till my services came to an end with the website. Once again, after a long time, I was reunited, with my teacher through the internet.

Of all the counselors of the forums I hosted online, Dr. Badri's was my favorite because I felt every week that he was genuinely helping people to solve their complex problems in life especially in a time when Muslims were beginning to be psychologically traumatized by the tragic events that were unfolding daily that were capable of engulfing them. Dr. Badri's style of counseling was very intimate and touching. Moreover, he was an expert in recognizing the maladies that afflict people by offering relevant and practical solutions to their problems. Unknown to Dr. Badri was the fact that at the time he was directly assisting others to heal their emotional woes, listening to his advice then also helped me get an emotional relief from matters that were troubling me at the time. Even though in his answers to people's questions he was not directly addressing me or the issues I was particularly facing, listening to him give therapy to others was therapeutically healing me as well. Dr. Badri's love that was conveyed in those sessions and the therapeutic power that love generated to heal everyone who was touched by it were but additional assets to his mastery of the science of human therapy. Now those sessions were collected in one format available to readers so that they may receive a share of that love and be healed by it. It brings me great joy to have participated in that endeavor with Dr. Badri and to see that it is being carried further to touch more people as it touched those who were its direct participants.

Omer Awass
American Islamic College, Chicago, Illinois, USA
May 2015.

Question 1
Lack of confidence and social anxiety

From Abu Talha

I wanted to ask you about the correct way of curing the problem of lack of self confidence. My childhood was not a stable one and my father spent most of the time shouting at the family and telling us all how useless we were. I still remember these childhood traumatic experiences and carry their hurt with me. But Alhamdulillah I have strong belief in Allah that helps me in my life but I still feel I am useless in comparison to others. I believe I am not intelligent and I am very forgetful and disorganized. I find it difficult to maintain orderliness and decorum. I try my best to worship Allah and to frequently pray in the mosque and I am active in da'wah but I always feel that other people are much more capable than me.

I struggle to fight my lack of self control but find it very difficult especially with food. If I ate much I felt depressed and feel ashamed. I feel bad about failing to control myself. I sometimes feel sad and depressed about my inability to be a devoted servant of Allah and to help my family. My lack of confidence holds me back from pushing the boundaries that other people do with full vigor and confidence. I am not really good at anything and I am worried about marrying and not being a good husband to my wife and passing on my bad traits to my children. I want to be a role model for my children but I feel inadequate. What steps can I take to try and build my confidence and be a good slave of Allah.

Forgive me if my question is so long.

Answer

It is an established fact now that the image that we have about ourselves is developed very early in our childhood. If the parents cause the child to feel socially undesirable or treat him harshly and tell him that he is useless or stupid the child will take these statements as true undisputable facts and will continue to consciously or unconsciously repeat these degrading thoughts to himself. These thoughts and beliefs will cause him or her to feel socially anxious and lose self confidence in himself as an adult. This fact, that our thinking is the generator of our feelings and emotions, is the cornerstone of cognitive therapy. And the influence of early childhood's negative cognitions is the specific area of schema-focused cognitive therapy. Some psychologists have even come up with the theory that this can be verified from a neuro-psychological point of view. They say that our left brain is responsible for our logical thinking while our right brain is that which triggers our emotions, feelings and sentiments. If the left brain becomes illogical and passes information to the right brain concerning the worth of the person, then the right brain, without questioning the validity of what has been referred to it, will automatically bring about the relevant demoting feelings and order the secretion of the hormones that are associated with a depressing mind-set and anxiety.

Your problem my son is that you have developed an illogical and untrue negative image of yourself. For years you have been consciously or unconsciously going over the demeaning statements that your father used to repeat to you. If you go through what you have written in your question such as saying that "You are not good at anything and that you feel useless and inferior to others" and that even in your future you expect to be a "failure as a parent and husband", you will discover the illogical nature of these assertions.

Our early Muslim scholars and physicians such as Ibn Qayyim Al-Jawziyyah and Al- Balkhi have stressed that this inner dialogue between a person and his soul is the main factor in shaping one's personality. Not only that, but they have discovered that some of these negative thoughts can be initiated by very quick reflections or inner whispers (*waswas*) that pass so quickly and stealthily through consciousness that the person fails to be aware of them. However, he or she would experience the negative emotions that they generate. The repetitive nature of these emotions causes the person to eventually accept them as beliefs about his personality. In this, our early Muslim scholars came up with the modern cognitive conception of automatic thoughts, the discovery of which is inappropriately attributed to Aaron Beck.

To cognitively treat your condition, you have to rationally question and challenge the validity of the negative thoughts you keep repeating to yourself. Your pessimistic beliefs about yourself eclipse the positive achievements in your life. For example, you mentioned that you are active and maybe successful in *da'wah*. I don't know much about your educational background, but it seems to me that you are or you were doing well in your university studies. I am also sure that if you look at the good things that you can do or the things that you have already done, you will be convinced about the irrationality of these negative thoughts that your father has implanted in your mind at a time when you used to look at him as a godfather and thus accepted his verdict without any shed of doubt.

You are a good Muslim. I recommend to you that whenever you are praying or contemplating about Allah's bounties on you, you should think positively about what you have accomplished and humbly offer your gratitude to Him. Be optimistic about what you plan to accomplish in future with His Divine support. Beg Him to bestow on you the tranquility and self-assurance that will give you the necessary motivation to pursue your *da'wah* and lead your private life with confidence. While in a serene and contemplative state of devotion and relaxed *tasbīh* imagine the spiritual blessings of God engulfing and supporting you. In this contemplative state, look at yourself from outside yourself and see how deceptive beliefs have undermined your self confidence.

Furthermore, I advise you to look for a good Muslim counselor or cognitive therapist who can help you to get rid of these negative thoughts and gradually train you to perform your tasks without fear or anxiety. These thoughts and feelings have entrenched themselves into your psyche for many years. This requires patience on your part to gradually replace them with rational positive thoughts and feelings. In my practice I have seen many patients who were suffering from chronic anxiety and ridden with crippling social phobias who dramatically improve in a few months with behavioral and spiritually oriented rational cognitive therapy.

A young female doctor suffering from pulmonary embolism

Question from a Sister

Assalamualaikum warahmatullah, I am a married, young female junior medical doctor. Normally I am physically fit and lead an active lifestyle. I have recently been been diagnosed with pulmonary embolism (blood clot/s) in the lungs which is a potentially fatal disease. *Alhamdulillah,* Allah the most Kind, Most Merciful has chosen me for this trial and I know that this is because of His love for me as it would either be to reward me or forgive my sins if I am patient. Indeed this trial is small in comparison to the trials Allah has inflicted upon many other Muslims. We don't know when we are going to die but now I know my risk of dying young is relatively high. Please give me some advice on how to carry on with my life in a balanced way that is optimistic and spiritually purposeful? This will enable me to be prepared to meet my Lord.

My second question is; what is *sakarat al-mawt*? Is it equivalent to something like a cardiac arrest or is it the pain experienced during the death of body cells out of deprivation of oxygen? Is *sakarat al-mawt* the stage just before the soul is pulled out of the body? I understand that the soul of the believers will be pulled gently by the angel of death; but at the same time *sakarat al-mawt* will be painful (as suffered by the Prophet (ṣ)). Please enlighten me on this. Also, my parents live in a faraway country. They are quite old. Should I tell them about my health? From the Islamic point of view, is it better for me not to tell them? If I tell them, they may be psychologically more prepared if anything happens to me. On the other hand, telling them would cause them to worry unnecessarily. Please make *du'ā'* for me and other Muslims to die as true believers.

Answer

I have been quite moved by your problem and I feel too humble to give you the advice you require. I wish only to remind you of the authenticated Hadith of the Prophet (ṣ) in which a black woman who was a companion of the Prophet (ṣ) complained to him that she suffered from epileptic seizures in which she lost consciousness and fell to the ground, sometimes exposing her body during her unconsciousness. She asked the Prophet (ṣ) to make *du'ā'* for her to be cured from her disease. The Prophet (ṣ) answered by saying that: "I can now make *du'ā'* for you and you will definitely be cured, but if you are patient enough to live with this disorder then I assure you that you will enter Paradise." The woman said, "O messenger of Allah I prefer to spend the rest of my life suffering from this disease and go to paradise; only make *du'ā'* for me that when I am unconscious I do not expose any part of my body that should be covered." The Prophet (ṣ) humbly supplicated asking Allah to grant her what she wanted. This woman lived for many years after the death of the Prophet (ṣ) and the companions of the Prophet will always point to her and say this is the women who will be admitted to paradise.

If we are to derive a lesson from this distinguished female companion, then I believe that I am not going beyond my limit if I give you good tidings that with the grace of Allah you are a woman of paradise if you continue to have the feelings and thoughts you have expressed in your question.

My dear daughter because of the influence of our modern materialistic life we consider death to be the end of life. In fact, death is only an elevated stage in which the soul is freed from the prison of time and space, which we are locked up in this life. I would like to mention to you a very interesting simile which Abu Hamid Al-Ghazali, the great Muslim sage (*Wali*), has mentioned in his magnum opus *Iḥyā' 'Ulūm al-Dīn*. I will try to modernize this example for you. He says that if we can talk to a fetus about to be born and if the fetus can understand what is said to it, it would not be able to imagine our description about the world outside the darkness of the womb. If we tell it about the moon and the sun, he/she cannot comprehend them because of his/her mind limitation and his inter uterine environment. During his/her life in the uterus of the mother the most important organ to him or her was the placenta which gives him/her nourishment and oxygen and takes away his/her waste products. After birth this placenta has no use for the baby. It is thrown away somewhere. From this moment until death, this world would take up the role of a very large uterus and the human body would assume the role that the placenta used to take when the fetus was in its intrauterine environment. If we are told in this world about life after death and the great things we will see in the *Barzakh* (intermediary stage between death and the afterlife) we will never be able to imagine them because we are like adult fetuses in the uterus of this life. When we die, we will no longer need our placental body. Our rebirth breaks the chains of the material world. In this way I imagine that our life is like a fired modern rocket. When it breaks the gravitational force, part of it will no longer have any use and it breaks off to free the essential component of the rocket to go faster to another planet.

So my dear daughter, though we fear death, it is in reality an experience which we should look forward to if we really wish to free our souls from the gravitational pull of the sinful material world. The process of birth is a painful experience for the baby as he is pushed out of his mother's uterus, but after that he/she is rewarded by a much richer and more meaningful life. Similarly, the process of dying is a painful experience leading to a much wider and unimaginable delightful existence. This should answer your question about *sakarat al-mawt*. It is a laboring rebirth for the Muslim to experience the amazing beauty of the friendly angels receiving the soul and giving him/her glad tidings and spiritual pleasures which are beyond the description of any human language. The Prophet (ṣ) endured the pain of death (*sakarat al-mawt*) more than the usual *mu'min* because of the spiritual station in Heaven he was travelling to was higher than any other spiritual station that could be experienced by any creation of Allah whether human or not.

Dear daughter your case reminds me of a Malaysian woman who shares your description in terms of dedication and love to Allah and to his Prophet (ṣ). She was suffering from cancer and during her painful terminal stage she refused to take any pain killers. She was saying that she did not want to drain her mind by taking drugs because she wanted to enjoy her last days in *istighfar* or asking for forgiveness and in the remembrance of Allah.

As for your parents, I cannot say definitively whether you should tell them or not. This may require the consent of somebody who knows more about their condition and is more learned in the Islamic religion than myself. So, if you have a wise relative living with your parents or near to them, he can gradually give them information about your health at the appropriate time and help them in managing their distress.

Lastly, my daughter, you know as a medical doctor that there are many cases of spontaneous remission of serious diseases which medical science cannot explain. I personally know of a doctor whose cancer was so advanced that it attacked his nervous system and he became paralyzed. His brother, sitting at his deathbed was continuously making *du'ā'* or praying for him, which he only stopped when he performed the obligatory daily prayers or when he took a little food or went to the bathroom. Professor Abu A'isha, a Professor of Medicine in the University of King Saud in Riyadh was taking care of this case. The patient gradually improved and in a few months, as Professor Abu A'isha stated, he was totally cured of his cancer. Modern medicine may call it spontaneous remission, but we know better. This case is confirmation of the verse in the Qur'an in which Allah says: "It is He who responds to the desperate one when he calls upon Him and removes his suffering".

Is the healing power of the mind over the sick body really true?

Question from Mithala

Can you please explain to me the meaning of the claim that the power of mind is capable of healing the body from disease and what is the Islamic point of view on this issue?

Answer

Allah created man from clay that developed into a body and a soul that is composed of the intangible spiritual aspects of his existence. Western secular science and medicine have unfortunately denied the existence of the soul or at least neglected its existence. They at times refer to it as mind and other times they call it psyche. The extremists among them will even deny the existence of a mind and they hope that in future a day will come when any sort of behavior that a person exhibits will be explained from the working of the brain and its electro-chemical activity.

Fortunately, there is now a growing number of a new generation of scientists who have discovered and shown the interaction between the human mind with its spiritual and non-material dimension that of his body. The evidence is too strong to be refuted. For example, a woman who is very anxious to have a baby may suddenly develop all of the symptoms and signs of pregnancy. Her period will stop, her breasts will enlarge, and her abdomen will increase in size showing the exact developmental stages of pregnancy. Even some doctors are at times deceived by this false pregnancy. In the University of Khartoum Hospital, I was told that such a false pregnancy was discovered only when the surgeon administered some tests before performing a cesarean surgery. In such cases we can see that the mind or soul has influenced the body in a dramatic manner. Once the woman realizes that she is not really pregnant, her body quickly returns to its normal form. Of course, secular scientists may continue to argue that it is only the electro-chemical activity of the brain which brings about such dramatic changes. But the evidence for a nonphysical mind or soul is accumulating.

From the Islamic point of view, this interaction between the soul and the body has been very clearly delineated by our early Muslim physicians such as Al-Balkhi, Ibn Sina, and Zakariya Al-Razi. They gained this knowledge from their in-depth studies of the Holy Qur'an and the aḥādīth of our Prophet (ṣ) that talk about the nature of man as having a body and soul interacting with each other. In fact to them, the word "mind" can be a synonym for soul since both are spiritual in nature.

Another Islamic evidence for the influence of the mind or soul over the body is that of supplication or *du'ā'*. Its influence is not limited to a Muslim praying for himself but also in helping to remove the suffering of another beloved person for whom we are praying. The benefit of supplication in healing the sick is now confirmed by modern controlled research studies in which the health of patients for whom some volunteers prayed for, improved more than those who were not prayed for even though these patients were unaware of being prayed for.

A young Muslim woman in love with an undeserving man

Question from Liza

I just heard of this site from a Muslim sister. I am going through a lot of pain at this time of my life and I thought that maybe you can help me. I met my boyfriend about two and half years ago. I wasn't a Muslim at the time. He was a senior and I was a freshmen. He helped in opening my heart to Islam, and we both converted. He converted before me and then joined the marines. I converted to Islam 6 months later. I thank Allah for sending him to me. But life isn't going as I planned. He left the marines and things started to change. I love him deeply and so does he. He moved to Florida and since we haven't seen each other in about four months he met another girl (not a Muslim) and has feelings for her. I am crushed. He says that he's going to drive to New York where I am living to see me again and to see how it is when we live together. If he feels that things could work out for us then he will be with me and leave her. But now it is becoming too long for me waiting for him. He is waiting for people to come with him. I love him so much. I am so sorry I am writing so much but I just need to let my feelings out. I don't have many Muslim friends and I live with a family whose members do a lot of *ḥarām* things. I think I should just wait for him to come and we talk. On top of what I said, he is now going out clubbing and has started to drink alcohol. He says that he needs me in his life to change him. He says he loves me and he can't get over me. He just needs to see me again. What should I do? I would appreciate it if you could respond. I have never been so hurt in my life. Thank you.

Answer

When a person converts to Islam, he/she would definitely go through a lot of challenges and problems. Some of these would be so painful that the person would feel like that he or she is holding a burning piece of coal in his/her hand. This analogy of the burning coal is not mine. This is what our Prophet (ṣ) said about people who practice their Islam at the end of time. There are many indications from the sayings of the Prophet (ṣ) and from the Qur'an that prove to us that we are indeed living at the end of time. So, my daughter Liza, your conversion in this anti-Islamic environment is a very blessed thing. You should be congratulated and given good tidings about Allah's Pleasure with you. Please do not bend or weaken in the face of these problems and challenges. The Qur'an tells us that we may love something very much, but it is eventually going to be bad for us. And we may dislike something very much and it will eventually be good for us. I believe that you are in love with a man who is probably not the right man for you and may not deserve the feelings that you have for him. For a young man to promise a lady that he wants to marry her and then go with another woman and indulge in drinking alcohol is clear evidence that he is immature and the foundations of his faith are not deeply rooted yet. I feel sure if you got married he may eventually deteriorate into excessive drinking or be infatuated with other women.

You are still young my dear daughter and falling in love creates a feeling in the lover that everything in their life is determined by this emotional relationship. This kind of love is the one that one loses after marriage. You spent a very short time together and you are both very young and may need time to mature. In such marriages, falling in love may soon be falling out of love. So if it didn't work out, it should not be the end of everything though it may temporarily appear as such to you now. However, I advise you to see him, but not with this emotional "crush". He is a man who first led you to Islam. Whether he is going to be your husband or not, it is your duty to help him as a Muslim brother. So I advise you to behave in a mature manner and to see him as a person who needs your help.

I also advise you to find some good Muslim friends who can support you and give you spiritual guidance in handling this challenge. May be Allah will send you a more Islamically committed young Muslim man with whom you can build a truly Muslim family.

Question 5

Comparing psychoanalysis with cognitive therapy

Question from Samah, UK

Can you discuss the major differences between the cognitive approach to psychotherapy and that of the Freudian school of psychoanalysis? Which approach is more accurate in the understanding of human behavior and which approach is closer to how Muslim scholars should deal with psychological disorders?

Answer

You must be a good student of psychology to have noticed that certain theories and practices are more un-Islamic than others. To understand the differences between the cognitive and the Freudian approaches to human behavior one would need to study the differences between these perspectives with respect to their conceptions about the nature of man. When Freud developed his psychoanalytic school as a theory of personality and a method of psychotherapy, he was greatly influenced by the anti-religious secular movement of the late nineteenth and early twentieth century. The open rebellion against the Church in earlier centuries brought about an extreme ideological retaliation that overturned the beliefs and doctrines of religion. Religion teaches that humans have souls and that they are responsible for whatever they do before God and that there is a Hereafter in which their actions will be judged. Accordingly, they must have freedom of choice to either act in a good way or in a sinful way.

As one of the leading founders of Western modernity and its new secular worldview, Freud denied the existence of God, the soul, the Hereafter and human free will. In preaching his new secular concept of man he had to invent a new godless ideology with a new "god". This new "god" is the unconscious. If man is motivated in whatever he does, from cradle to grave, by unconscious forces then he does not have the freedom to choose. And since Freud postulated that the unconscious is propelled by sexual and aggressive impulses, the whole conception of sinful and evil behavior that religion teaches became challenged.

One of the main reasons why Freud was hailed as a hero by Western societies at that time was because he gave them a good justification for their emancipation from the dogmatism of Catholicism and his creation of a psychotherapeutic technique that attempted to fill the vacuum created by the downfall of the church. For example, sinners who used to confess to a priest and feel better after being blessed and forgiven, now confess to an analyst who convinces them that their behavior is unconsciously motivated and that after all there is no such thing as sin or divine punishment. They then feel relieved!

By overstressing sex and aggression as the motivators of all sorts of human behavior, psychoanalysis has deprived man of his rational conscious motivation. Western psychology had to wait for the cognitive revolution to regain its concept of mind and the important role of conscious motivation. This is so, because the other rival schools which dominated Western psychology such as behaviorism had also played down the importance of conscious motivation and the role of the mind in decision making and in the development of emotions. So, though behaviorism disagreed with Freud, its proponents considered the environment as the main creator and to some, the sole player in the development of human personality and action. They came up with the influential paradigm of limiting their studies to stimuli and their responses (S-R psychology) without caring to study the internal conscious processes that make a person decide what response to carry out with respect to the different stimuli he receives in his environment. They were misled into believing that this will make psychology a real science. But of course they fully agreed with Freud with respect to his staunch negative attitude to religion.

By freeing man from the tyranny of Freudian unconscious and behavioral 'scientism', cognitive psychology came to bring us back the age-old conception of the supremacy of human conscious thinking in developing our mental and emotional reactions. This cognitive approach was the one time followed by early Muslim physicians and psychologists in treating patients of various emotional disorders. They believed firmly that it is not the things that directly cause us to be emotional but it is the way we look at things which causes us to react emotionally. So they considered human conscious thinking as the original cause of emotional responses. Their therapy was directed toward changing the thought of the person so that his/her emotions will automatically follow from those healthy changes in thoughts. In this respect, if you read or check in the internet the translation of the manuscript titled *Sustenance of Body and Soul* written by Abu Zayd Al-Balkhi more than 12 centuries ago, you will find that the acclaimed contributions of pioneers of modern cognitive therapy such as Beck and Ellis has already been preceded.

Modern cognitive psychology is clearly more Islamic than other approaches in psychology. That is so because if our beliefs and thoughts are the ones that generate our healthy or unhealthy emotions, then in treating a Muslim patient therapists must concentrate their healing efforts on the religious beliefs of Muslim patients whether they are committed to Islam or not. In my own clinical practice, I have always found that using this Islamic oriented cognitive therapy effective in bringing about dramatic improvement in patients who failed to respond to psychiatric treatment with drugs or to psychoanalytic and psychodynamic therapies. In fact, some of my patients who had been treated with psychoanalytically oriented therapy had deteriorated after 'therapy'. For example, a pious but simple Saudi young man who was referred to a psychoanalyst for helping him with his generalized anxiety disorder became worse after the analyst informed him that his anxiety is due to suppressed and repressed sexuality and that to be better he must have a girlfriend. The patient came to consult me about his generalized anxiety plus the newly acquired serious feelings of guilt, moral confusion and depression. He sadly expressed his moral dilemma as a Muslim who believes that fornication is declared a sinful act by Allah while the 'science of psychotherapy' recommends it as a means of attaining relief from neurotic disorder. If that is the case, then one of them, either prohibition against fornication by God or being permitted to have sex to cure psychological disorder must be wrong! It took time to first 'treat' his ideological conflict and then his generalized anxiety disorder.

Another issue that exacerbates the symptoms of Muslim patients referred to analysts is that the therapy by free association can cause them to remember very painful repressed experiences such as being sexually abused as a child by a relative. This will naturally increase their anxiety and anger or make them feel worthless and hopeless. It would have been better for them not to remember these unconscious experiences. The paradigm popularized by Freud that no real improvement will happen unless unconscious material is made conscious is not correct in most cases. I hope that you will in future be able to become a good cognitive therapist in your western country where Muslim patients are struggling to find Muslim therapists who understand their spiritual and unique psychological problems.

Are possessions by jinn that lead to seeing things or hearing voices real or are merely psychological and mental disorders?

Question from Fatima

I was just wondering about the Islamic view versus the psychological view on being possessed by jinn to the extent of seeing things and hearing voices. Are all claimed possessions by jinn real or symptoms of psychological disorders?

Answer

This issue is now being discussed in various psychological perspectives in the Islamic and Western worlds. A few years ago, the idea of a spirit possessing a human being was completely rejected by western psychologists. They stamp it as a form of a superstitious belief carried over from the Middle Ages. However, as science became fully established and mature, a few mental health professionals started to re-examine the possibility of such a phenomenon and to study spiritual healing with an open mind. In the 1980's I was elected as a member of the World Health Organization Committee on traditional medical practices. In one meeting in Geneva we listened to doctors and researchers who delivered a number of papers in which they documented the dramatic improvement of patients in Africa and Asia who were treated by spiritual healers who practiced exorcism and alternative spiritual therapy. One Nigerian physician reported that after failing to help some of his terminally ill patients, he was astonished to find that they regained their health after being treated by traditional healers. This motivated him to study the spiritual therapy of these healers. He was not only convinced about the efficacy of their therapy but he decided to abdicate his modern medical practice and to become a spiritual traditional healer. My own research was on traditional healing in Ethiopia and Sudan. I have also reported on similar cases.

In general, some of those who are considered possessed by traditional healers as being possessed by evil spirits are the ones who are diagnosed by psychiatrists as suffering from schizophrenia or mania. The diagnostic term "schizophrenia" is a very ambiguous label and psychiatrists stick it on anybody who exhibits the symptoms of delusions or false beliefs or who suffers from hallucinations in which he/she sees things that are not really there or hears voices from invisible beings. In my study I listened to Muslim healers who strongly criticized this broad classification of mental illness. They say that to consider anybody schizophrenic only because he/she sees things and hears voices, is like a doctor who says that all patients who have fever, headache and nausea must be suffering from malaria. Since a high fever and headache can be caused by so many illnesses, to stick to one diagnosis is neither rational nor scientific. The same applies, as these healers argue, to the concept of schizophrenia. In fact, medically hallucinations can be caused by disorders other than the accepted biochemical imbalance in the brain such as alcoholic poisoning, dementia, delirium or some other reasons. So why can we not have an open mind to also consider a spiritual cause in the diagnosis of mental illness?

The traditional healers also claim that the main evidence for the biochemical theory of schizophrenia is that patients improve when they are given the prescribed drug or by receiving electro-convulsive therapy, but they also argue that at least a quarter or more of them do not improve. They are permanently kept in mental hospitals as chronic schizophrenics. These healers argue that if improvement is the evidence, then they have a number of cases of chronic schizophrenics who responded to their therapy in a much shorter time.

Furthermore, spiritual healers state that some dedicated worshippers can hear voices and see things that others do not see or hear but they are quite sane. What they see and hear beyond time and space is always confirmed in real life. In fact hearing voices should not always be diagnosed as an auditory hallucination as psychiatrists quickly wish to diagnose. At the personal level, I have a relative who frequently hears a voice calling his name. He exhibited no other psychological or mental disorder. He was a very popular teacher in a village school. He told me that at one late night a group of his colleagues decided to pay him an expected visit since he was living alone but they found his outside door already locked. They could see him walking around in his sitting room since the outside wall is not high. So they shouted to him to open his door. Very loudly, they yelled, "Hassan ... Hassan" but he didn't even look at the direction where they are. He thought that it was the usual voice calling his name. In the morning at school, he found them angry at him. "We loudly called out to you but you intentionally ignored us"; he could not tell them the truth because they may think he was mad!

In May 2001 a very interesting conference was held in

Dammam, Saudi Arabia in which psychiatrists and well-known traditional Muslim healers discussed the value of *ruqaiyyah* (prayer for therapeutic purposes as well as exorcism of jinn possession). I took part in this conference and I was happy to see western-trained Arab psychiatrists accepting the possibility of jinn possession and showing their readiness to cooperate with Muslim healers by referring to them as those who do not benefit from their modern psychiatric therapy. Therefore, as Muslims, we should not dismiss the possibility of jinn possession. We have in the traditions of our prophet (s) and the biography of early Muslim physicians much evidence to the therapeutic benefit of reading verses from the Holy Qur'an as a form of exorcism. We should be open minded in accepting the physical as well as the spiritual aspects of human nature.

But it is very important for those who accept exorcism not to treat those possessed as sinful or deviant persons. Just as the body may develop a disorder, the soul can also be disordered. However, I wish to bring to your attention the fact that in our culture many psychologically and mentally disordered patients are quickly 'diagnosed' by their relatives as being spiritually attacked by jinn. They take them to Muslim traditional healers who fail to help them. Most of these patients could have been cured or much improved by drugs or psychotherapy but their disinclined relatives deprive them of the beneficial modern therapy.

A conflict between a demanding wife and her mother in law

Question from Arif

My wife disrespects with my mother and ill-treats her. She behaves nicely with me sometimes and sometimes not. She has a very deep rooted psychological problem and if she does not like someone it is hard to make her like that person. She at times prevents me from taking care of my mother. My mother is old and my father is dead. My other two brothers take care of my mother and they live in a different house. My wife's father and I have talked to my wife several times to change her ways, but she won't and she cannot. She would cry and be depressed the whole time if she is forced to do something. Please advise me.

Answer

I do not think you need me to reiterate the Islamic injunction of kindness towards parents in general and mothers in particular. The Qur'an has instructed us that when our parents become old, we should not frown on them or demean towards them. You say that your wife cannot change her heart if she dislikes somebody. You should not ask her to change what's in her mind, but you should ask her to change her disrespectful behavior. Since your mother is not living with her, she should at least tolerate her and behave nicely towards her during the brief period in which your mother visits you or when you go to visit her. If you feel that your wife is probably suffering from depression or some other neurotic disorder then try to convince her to seek therapy. But you should not allow her to use her mood swings to be an excuse for her to ill treat your mother.

Also try to talk to your mother gently to make an effort to treat your wife nicely like her daughter. Tell your mother that your wife is not emotionally well and that she needs to be helped. Try to reduce the state of tension and mistrust between them in a way that is tactful. For example, you can tell your wife that your mother said she is a good and beautiful woman and tell your mother that your wife praises her a lot. If all your efforts do not succeed, do not submit to her attempts to prevent you from taking care of your mother. You mentioned that at times she does that. You have to fulfill your Islamic duty to your mother whether she likes it or not.

Question 8
A case of bipolar disorder

Question from Zee

I have bipolar disorder and I was wondering whether it is alright to take medication for it. Also what medication do you recommend that has the least side effects?

Answer

Bipolar disorder was previously and more appropriately known as manic depressive psychosis. It is a mood disorder in which the patient suffers from serious swings of mood between mania and depression. If you were correctly diagnosed, you must have noticed that during the manic phase you used to have extremely optimistic and unrealistic beliefs about your abilities. Thoughts raced through your mind causing you to jump from one thought to the other. You were extremely active without feeling tired and you needed little sleep. When the antithetical mood of depression occurred, you must have had the opposite symptoms. You were feeling sad, tired and generally retarded and slowed down physically and mentally. You became pessimistic and you lost interest in life and its pleasures.

You asked whether you should take medications. Yes you must. Zee, please quickly seek the help of a psychiatrist to prescribe suitable medications such as mood stabilizing drugs or some other physical treatment for you. The earlier you start treatment, the better chances you have for improvement. So please do not delay getting this help. Unlike anxiety disorders such as phobias and obsessive-compulsive disorders or milder forms of depression, that can be helped with psychotherapy and cognitive behavior therapy without necessarily taking drugs, the treatment of bipolar disorder depends mainly on drugs and physical therapy. The issue of choosing the best medication for a patient is not an easy matter. There is no major medication for psychiatric patients that does not cause some form of side effects. Moreover, people differ a lot with respect to their response to different kinds of drugs. Furthermore, making the correct diagnosis for bipolar disorder may need an experienced psychiatrist since some other diseases such as thyroid disorders and borderline personality disorder may mimic or appear with symptoms similar to that of bipolar disorder. On top of that, bipolar disorder can come with full blown mania or with another milder form known as hypomania. After you improve with psychiatric therapy then you can seek the assistance of psychotherapists or counselors who can help you to cope with the difficulties of the disorder. Such therapists can educate you and your family members in helping you to develop a healthy style of life. As Muslims, we generally have caring family members and friends who are willing to patiently offer you the support and the time you need. Finally, you can benefit from the spiritual therapy of a pious Muslim healer. In my research on traditional medical practices in the Sudan, I have witnessed their significant psycho-spiritual healing abilities. May Allah help you dear Zee to get the correct diagnosis and treatment.

Question 9
A good Muslim suffering from homosexual fantasies

Question from Abu Yusuf

I am a 38-year-old Arab living in Berlin, a graduate of an Islamic university. Please help me to cure myself. I love men. I do not love women. My sexual thoughts are only about men. I did not have any sexual intercourse in my life, but I am very tired because of these bad thoughts. It is a very serious ordeal or *fitnah*. What can I do? Am I created this way?

Answer

Your problem is not an uncommon one and it can be helped if you find the suitable cognitive behavior therapist in your country. However, for the success of therapy, it is very important for you my dear brother not to despise yourself or feel unduly guilty about these sexual feelings. Since you have not intentionally put this deviant lust into your mind, if you hate and resist it, Allah will bestow His reward upon you. So instead of misery, it can be a source of spiritual blessing. I wish to discuss this issue in a detailed but simplified manner because western modernity has created much confusion in the minds of the Muslim and other youth brought up in different religious and cultural backgrounds.

Many young Muslims have asked the same question.

In the sixties and early seventies behavior therapists developed a successful therapy for homosexual feelings and practices that was based on learning by conditioning. This was what is known as aversion therapy. They generally used pictures or slides of naked males and as soon as a measuring device showed that the person had become sexually aroused, he was given an electric shock or some other aversive punishment such as an offensive smell or a drug that caused him to feel nauseated. After this, he is shown pictures or films of seductive women and he was asked to sexually fantasize and to develop positive sexual tendencies towards them. Some therapists used to quickly alternate pictures of males and females. The shock or punishment was given only when a male picture was presented. Instead of this physical pain, some of the therapists relied on imagined aversive and disgusting scenes and a cognitive approach such as showing the bad aspects of this sexual behavior. Of late, therapists have been applying more of cognitive than classical behavior therapy.

My dear brother, you are living in Berlin, so do not be influenced by the biased authors and by the western media that keep repeating the myth of the heritability of homosexuality as if it were an established scientific fact; as if some people are biologically created to be homosexuals and no therapy can change a biological predisposition. This is nonsense. There is no gay gene; all the biased researches that tried to come up with such beliefs have failed to do so. Allah is just; He will not put such hypothetical genes or hormones into a person and then punish him for acting according to the inherited characteristics that He created in him. You were not biologically created to have this lust. It must have developed from some experiences or wrong information that you may or may not remember. If homosexuality were an inherited human trait, it would have been found in all parts of the globe. This is obviously not so. In many tribes in Africa and Asia homosexuality is unknown.

Some gay activists claim that the difference between men and women is large enough to bring about this inherited sexual preference; but what about the difference between adults and little boys and girls? Why doesn't this much larger difference develop into an inherited pedophilia or sexual lust for children? Why are there no professionals who speak about the heritability of pedophilia; simply because it is a repulsive practice that violates the western cultural norms. Or for that matter, why don't we hear about an inherited sexual desire for animals? It is obviously because animals cannot complain in court!

We as Muslims and as committed Christians should realize that modern Western secular humanism that brought about the contemporary sexual revolution will continue to wage its *jihad* with the hope of establishing homosexuality in the whole wide world. Look at the way how Western modernity induced its academicians and its powerful media to gradually desensitize its citizens to accept homosexuality. First, when Christianity was still respected, it was looked at as a sin and was properly named "sodomy". Then it became an abnormal deviant sexual disorder that needed to be treated and not a sinful practice. So the term changed to homosexuality. The tag of sinfulness disappeared and homosexuals became patients. This continued until 1973 when the gay activists pressured the American Psychiatric Association to remove homosexuality from its list of psychiatric disorders. With time, the term "gay" became more popular and many westerners began to see gays as sexually variant and not sexually deviant. And as gays felt more confident, they moved from a defensive to an offensive strategy. They came up with a new term, "homophobia", to stamp people who showed hate or fear or who discriminated against homosexuals. According to this 'psychopathological diagnosis', if anyone refuses to accept gays or takes an emotional stand against them, he or she must seek psychological help for this irrational phobia!

Accordingly, interest in treating gays gradually waned and funding scientific research on finding better methods of therapy in this area became dearth. Changing the sexual orientation of gays by aversion therapy was prohibited by the American Psychological Association and some of its extreme members wanted to illegalize any attempt to change same sexuality to heterosexuality!

This offensive strategy is now being internationalized by Western powers defending homosexuals in 'homophobic' countries like Zimbabwe, Uganda and Nigeria where this deviant practice is legally prohibited and frowned upon. America, the chief defender of gays criticizes these Africans for preventing men and women from their human right of sexual enjoyment! They even threatened some African countries that illegalized homosexuality and same sex marriages by withholding Western financial aid. To me, this is one of the most extreme forms of ethical ethnocentrism. The term "ethnocentrism" stands for those who arrogantly believe that their culture and ethical values are the only righteous and blameless ones and that all other groups should follow their ways.

I lived among the Dinka tribe in South Sudan in the early eighties. Homosexuality was not only nonexistent but they did not have a word for it in their language. I found a similar situation when I lived among the rural people of Bahardar in Ethiopia in 1973. Many Africans would look at homosexuality the way westerners would see incest or pedophilia. An African man will be surprised to know that in the US he would be imprisoned if he married a 17-year-old girl who matured since she was 13 but he would be congratulated if he marries an 18-year-old boy.

So my dear Abu Yusuf this is the situation in Europe and you have to bravely fight the cultural and ethical prejudices in seeking the proper therapy. Psychologists and psychiatrists from the Catholic Medical Association are among the few professional therapists who successfully swam against the libertine currents. Since they do not subscribe to the ethics of the sexual revolution, they are highly successful in treating Christians who wish to be treated from their gay practices and fantasies. They use cognitive behavioral techniques and aversion therapy. If you find a committed Muslim therapist, he can combine his cognitive behavior therapy with an Islamic therapeutic approach. Aversion therapy is useful and illegalizing its use is not rational since many Western therapists still use it in treating other disorders. In the late sixties and early seventies, I have personally applied a form of aversion therapy combined with Islamic spiritual cognitive therapy in treating Muslim homosexuals. All those who were strongly committed to the treatment benefited from my therapy.

I clearly remember two of them because their improvement was dramatic. One of them was an Arab diplomat. He was only sexually aroused by very black men with bad odor. His elderly parents wanted him to get married soon in order to see his children before they died. This is usually a sentimental tactic employed by old parents to coerce their children to get married. He first resisted the pressure from his parents, but later accepted to propose to engagement with a beautiful fiancé whom his parents selected for him. He reported that he used to hold her hand and hug her without feeling any sexual desire. In a few sessions of aversion and Islamic cognitive spiritual therapy he was able to be sexually attracted to his fiancé and with more sessions he was successful in having intercourse after marriage. Like you, he had the deviant lust but he never actualized it. So your condition is treatable since our sexuality is mainly determined by our environment and there is no learnt human habit that cannot be changed by unlearning and by habit substitution. I advise you to look for a beautiful wife. Nowadays, you do not need much money to get married. Many widows and divorcees in Berlin would be happy to get married to you. Since you have not had any sexual intercourse before, the therapy plus the joy of having sex with a woman would most certainly make you have a strong desire for a normal heterosexual relationship.

A woman who inappropriately blames herself

Question from Huda

The husband of my friend committed suicide after she left him. He was violent and cruel towards her and their children. He had some kind of psychological illness related to depression. Now his family is blaming her for his death and she feels guilty about it. What can she do to be relieved from this feeling of guilt?

Answer

Please tell your friend that her husband had been suffering from a serious psychotic disorder. I suspect that he used to be a suspicious person obsessed with delusions that at times accompanied this psychotic behavior. Divorcing him was definitely a wise decision at that time. If he continued to live with her and the children he would have caused them much psychological harm. The fact that he committed suicide showed that her decision was correct. The feeling of his parents, though natural, is a selfish response. They are only thinking about their son and not compassionately looking at the welfare of the wife and family as whole. Your friend and the parents of the deceased should have a firm belief in *Qadar* (predestination). The suicide of the man was not caused by anybody let alone the abused wife. He could have committed suicide after killing the wife or causing more harm to the children. Therefore she should not have feelings of guilt over something that she had no control over. If she continues to say to herself that had I not left him he would not have died, she would be vulnerable to negative thoughts that might eventually cause her to become depressed. She should consider what had happened could not have been avoided and she should look optimistically to her relationship with Allah and to the possibility of remarrying and having a happy life.

Islam and psychology

Question from Shahzeb

I am a student. I have always been wondering how Islam views modern psychology.

Answer

This is a very broad topic be discussed in detail in such a forum. However, I shall give you a few general ideas. Many Muslim students shy away from psychology because they wrongly believe it may confuse them and undermine their faith. Most of them had read or heard scanty information about Sigmund Freud and his psychoanalytic theories. They think that all psychology is Freudian in nature. Ironically, though Freud is the most famous in this field, his psychoanalysis is not part of academic psychology. Furthermore, recent research in the history of psychology has discredited Freud and his works. Famous researchers have exposed his deceptiveness and have shown the influence of Jewish mystical traditions on his theories. Of late, it has been reported that his bizarre theories on the exaggerated role of sex in motivating all forms of human behavior were written when he was under cocaine addiction. Accordingly, a number of British universities now teach Freud only as history of psychology.

Another important fact that should encourage young Muslims to study psychology is that it is really not a solid, coherent logically arranged discipline that can challenge their cherished beliefs. It is not really a science in the manner that students think of science. Psychology can be viewed as an exact science only when it merges with exact sciences. For example physiological psychology, genetic psychology, psycho-pharmacology, perception and learning are in a 'no man's land' with biology and chemistry and other sciences. These disciplines have no problem with Islam as a religion. In fact studying these disciplines can make one a better Muslim if he or she contemplates upon the great creation of Allah in His human servants.

However when psychology merges with philosophy and is influenced by the ethical values of Western modernity it becomes a culture bound subject stuffed with pseudo-scientific material. The Western worldview is based on secular anti-religious conceptions about the nature of man and his existence. This is not science. Neither Freud, nor Watson nor Rogers nor any of the founders of modern psychology had closed himself in experimenting in a laboratory to come up with the results that man is driven by sexual impulses or that he is just an animal or that he has a selfish aggressive nature. We as Muslim students of psychology should learn to discriminate between the useful aspects of modern psychology supported by true science and the collection of unverified theories that is a natural product of a culture without a soul. The confusion to Muslim students is actually not caused by psychology as a subject, but by their psychology lecturers who teach them all the material of psychology as if it were a true 'science'. They do not teach their students to distinguish between the sexual theory of the "Oedipus

Complex" of Freud and his other weird ideas as compared with the verified influence of chromosomal abnormalities on human behavior. However, there is a growing interest among Muslim psychologists to Islamize these fields of specialization so that Western psychology can be de-secularized or 'de-kafirized'.

A case of unwarranted feelings of guilt

Question from Sahar

I am in a desperate situation. About 10 years ago I fell in love with a man and he also fell in love with me. I was happy about being in love because this was like a success story for me. Maybe my past was also influential because I thought that no one would fall in love with me. Everything was fine until he proposed to me. He knew that I love him and will not refuse his proposal, but I rejected him because I realized that he would not be a suitable husband. When I rejected him, he was shocked and angry and told me it was my fault, because if I hadn't expressed my love he would not have come towards me (I think he was right).

From then onward I started to feel guilty and I decided to punish myself, I developed severe headaches and sadness and anxiety and I couldn't study. Recently I got married. My husband is a good man but unfortunately he is a close friend of him. Now 10 years have passed but I still suffer from feelings of guilt and still couldn't concentrate. Now my feeling of guilt and sinfulness are like an obsession. Whatever I want to do, these thoughts come up to block my mind. I repeat to myself that I committed a sin and I hurt a person. I asked Allah to forgive me but I am still constantly tormented by these thoughts.

He is not married yet and he has girlfriends. When he visits my husband he says out loud that he hates to get married. I am also punished by the thought that if he makes an unsuccessful marriage it will be my fault. I feel that Allah is punishing me. May be I should accept this since it may reduce my greater punishment in the Hereafter. So I should be patient and not ask for a cure. However, if I get no cure, I can't live and work normally. So my situation is so tormenting that it is affecting my life. Please help me and tell me what to do. Should I get help to stop these obsessive thoughts and if I do so am I working against God's punishment?

Thank you for your help, I need it very much.

Answer

First of all, I think that your problem is caused by your misconception about the nature of our beloved creator, Allah *Subhanahu wa Ta'ala*. You are an extremely sensitive woman who can easily blame herself for things that she might not have done. With this emotional sensitivity, you conceived that Allah has no business but to wait for his slaves to do something wrong so He can quickly punish them. Relax after prayers and deeply contemplate in the Blessed names of Allah as the loving God, the Merciful and the Forgiver of sins. The Prophet (ṣ) says that Allah says that if you as humans do not commit sins, then He will remove you from the surface of the earth and create other beings that sin so He will forgive them. This belief is very important for those who commit *kaba'ir* or great sins such as stealing or fornication. But my dear Sahar have not committed a sin in all what you said? No you have not in the way you have described it to me.

The second misconception is with regards to your belief in destiny. Belief in *Qadar* or destiny is a cornerstone of Islam. Whether what happens to you in this life is good and pleasurable or whether it is bad and painful is already preordained and recorded. You cannot avoid it. Read the Hadith in which the Angel Jibrīl came to our Prophet in human form and asked him,

"What is *iman*"? The Prophet (ṣ) mentioned belief in *Qadar* just after belief in Allah and His angels and His prophets and His revealed books. So my dear daughter the fact that you refused to marry this man is something that has been already destined before you were born and even before you came to this earth. It is neither a mistake nor a sin to show a positive feeling towards a man but later feel that he is not the right husband for you. As I said, you are too sensitive and you have little confidence in yourself. Your feeling towards him was partly a form of gratitude for his love to you because you wrongly thought because of your lack of self-confidence that men may not be interested in you. You were wrong since another man came quickly after he left. So you should train yourself not to believe in the negative thoughts that you conditioned yourself to accept. You should build your self-confidence.

The third point which I understand from your question is that you have an extreme sense of pessimism about yourself and your environment to the extent that you have developed an un-Islamic Catholic approach about a wish to be punished. If you look at the whole situation optimistically and have a strong belief in Allah and His *Qadar*, then you would have seen a lot of good in being saved from a marriage that might have started with excessive love that would soon end after the passage of time. It seems to me that this person whom you refused to marry is rather immature and that he would have been a bad husband to you. For a man to refuse to marry all his life just because a woman once refused to marry him is not a sign of an emotionally grown-up person. With optimism you will also look at the good attributes of your current husband and you will be able to thank Allah and unburden yourself from the heavy load you voluntarily placed on yourself. With this new optimistic spirit you don't need to avoid seeing your former beloved and have a good relationship with his family if he already has one.

According to what I have said, Sahar, you have not committed a sin by refusing to marry your former beloved. This excessive feeling of guilt you are experiencing may also be a form of concealed depression. If after you change your attitude and that of your social environment, you continue to suffer from this uncalled for guilt then maybe you may need to see a Muslim psychiatrist or counselor to help you overcome this disorder.

Question 13

The danger of unnecessarily delaying marriage

Question from Yousef

What should a person do if he wants to marry early, that is at 20. If he doesn't he may not be able to keep his chastity for long? However, his parents are not ready to help him to get married.

Answer

Your problem is actually one that most young men and women suffer from. We as a Muslim nation have brought this problem you mentioned on ourselves by accepting Western concept of the development of human beings. Western society has gone from one extreme philosophical view to another with respect to the conception of what a child is. In the past centuries, the child since early childhood was looked at as a miniature adult. He is dressed like an adult and was obliged to work in industries like adult workers. Then when they realized their mistake, they went to the other extreme view about the nature of human development by considering young adults as children up to the age of 18 and sometimes even until the age of 21. The whole educational, economic, social, and judicial systems are based on this new conception. So a typical westerner does not marry and bear the responsibility of family at the age of twenty. He would be a student in the high school or university and he would need years to graduate and become economically independent. For this system to function, Western society has to allow teenagers and young adults to freely engage in sexual relations.

We as Muslims foolishly adopted their system, but continued to attempt to uphold Islamic ethical moral values governing the relationship between sexes. In Islam a person is considered an adult as soon as he/she reaches the stage of puberty. Our Islamic history tells us that young men at the age of 14 and 15 were already married and that young men like the illustrious companion of the Prophet (ṣ) Osama bin Zaid was appointed as the general of the Muslim army in which some of the dignitaries and the companions were mere soldiers. At that time, he was less than 18 lunar years old, so he was less than 17 years old by the solar calendar.

My dear son, I do appreciate your problem, but we cannot do much if your parents continue to adhere to their current position which is based on modern Western society's cultural values. I personally believe that it would not be a big issue if we allow our children to get married and we can ask them to postpone having children until they have the economic means of supporting their families.

My dear son, if you feel that the sexual urge is causing you much distress, then you must realize by resisting these sexual urges to please your parents in not getting married you are getting a lot of reward from Allah and you must derive satisfaction from this. Secondly, you can follow the injunction of the Prophet (ṣ) for those who are undergoing the same problem as you by voluntary fasting (*Siyam*). The act of fasting will curb your sexual urges. Also, try to avoid seeing films and videos that exacerbate your sexual urges. Finally, you must spend more time in spiritual and extra devotional activities such as offering voluntary prayers, Islamic contemplation (*Tafakur*). In addition, another way of relieving sexual tension is through physical exercise and engaging in interesting hobbies and volunteer work that would make your life more productive and meaningful.

Son, we live in a bad time which is full of sexual enticement that is directed to the young. Wherever the young man looks he will see something that tempts him to commit fornication. We also live in the time of HIV/AIDS for which there is no cure or vaccine. It is because of postponement of marriage during the long wait of postponement of marriage until finishing university studies, renting or purchasing a flat and buying a car that young Muslims succumb to fornication and get the lethal infection. This bad choice unfortunately makes them vulnerable to infection by sexually transmitted diseases or more seriously by HIV infection. So do not submit to the temptation of committing *zina*. It is authenticated that a young man complained to Ibn Abbas the learned uncle and companion of our noble Prophet (ṣ) that he was suffering from an irresistible sexual urge and that he masturbated to relieve this unbearable tension. Ibn Abbas told him that what he did is better than fornication. For this reason, the various Islamic schools '*Madhahib*' do not consider masturbation a prohibited act. Some consider it as an act that is frowned upon or *makruh* but not prohibited or *ḥarām*. All the claimed *aḥādīth* or sayings of the Prophet that are popularly quoted to condemn masturbation are certainly not authenticated and some of them are even fabricated. We also know now from modern medicine that all the invented physical and mental disorders that are supposed to afflict the masturbator are not real.

The westerners have solved the sexual problems of their young people by the practice of boys having girlfriends and girls having boyfriends and the Muslim *Shī'ah* sect has come up with the practice of temporary marriage of *mut'ah*. It is mainly our *Sunni* Muslim youth who have no alternative. Muslim *Sunni* clerics who often choose the most extreme decrees or *fatwas* do not really appreciate the unfulfilled sexual urges of young and adolescent Muslims, since most of these clerics are polygamous and enjoy a sexually satisfying life!

A case of obsessive-compulsive disorder regarding religious aspects

Question from Azhar

In the last seven years I have been suffering from insinuating thoughts about Allah, the Prophet, Islam *etc.* (*waswas*). I am trying very hard to get rid of this problem but I have not been able to do so. I contemplated committing suicide many times in order to be permanently free from these evil thoughts, but then I also thought that this is not allowed in Islam. I consulted many physiatrists who gave me certain medications but they did not help much. I have been told that it is an illness called OCD (Obsessive-Compulsive Disorder). After that I consulted number of scholars about this problem and they told me that it is a demonic possession, *shaitan*. Sometimes I feel that I might have gone out of Islam. Would you please help me with some remedy?

Answer

I would like you to view this obsessive-compulsive disorder as a test or (*ibtila'*) from Allah. Some people are tested by physical illness, some are tested with loss of money or life of relatives and some like you are tested with psychological disorders. The most important thing I would like you to know is that your feeling of anxiety and guilt is a very clear indication of your strong faith in

Allah or your *Iman*. Had it not been for the fact that you value your relationship with Allah, you wouldn't have had any psychological pain regarding these thoughts. A person who loses his faith in Allah will enjoy leading a sinful life – life without having any guilt or shame. He may indulge in taking alcohol and fornicating like a happy-go-lucky atheist. So take your symptoms as evidence to your strong belief.

Though modern psychiatry considers OCD to be one of the most difficult neurotic disorders with respect to its treatment, most patients greatly improve with a combination of drugs and psychotherapeutic treatment. I have personally helped such OCD patients by the use of exposure and response prevention therapy, relaxation, systematic desensitization, and aversion therapy to their unwanted thoughts. A good Muslim psychologist can explain to you the nature of these therapies and he can combine them with spiritual therapy to help you out of this dilemma.

When you stand up to pray and you experience these ugly obsessional thoughts attacking your mind, do not feel dejected. Though you may not know it, the prayers you offer while being troubled with these obsessions are in fact more accepted and rewarded by Allah than the prayers of many people who do not suffer from this disorder. Allah is aware of your agony and He will reward you for that. This optimistic approach will help you much in reducing the severity of these obsessive negative thoughts. Let the ugly thoughts continue without disturbing you too much. Let them come and go as they wish while you are busy doing your job. You must know that even the companions of the Prophet (ṣ) used to have fleeting thoughts of disbelief and *kufr*. They used to say it would be better for one to be thrown from the top of the mountain of Uhud in Medina and break his neck than to express these thoughts openly. When they complained to the

Prophet (ṣ) about these thoughts, he smiled and told them that is the evidence for their *Iman* (faith).

Hence, you should know that the difference between you and other psychologically healthy Muslims is a difference of the degree of these evil thoughts. Every Muslim gets some of these thoughts, at times in his/her prayer, but they are not greatly disturbed by them. The frequency of these thoughts and their severity reach their highest level when they cause the person to have a disorder like yours. From my experience in treating OCD related to religion, I found that it is better for the patient to say his prayers with other Muslims in *Jam'ah* instead of praying alone. He or she will get the spiritual benefit of congregational prayer and will have no doubts about the correctness of performing the rituals. Furthermore, I advise you to actively participate in activities that are interesting to you and to avoid being alone or solitary as much as possible. Find a good friend who can preoccupy your time with good and amusing companionship.

Undue anxiety

Question from Judith, Canada

Alhamdulilah, I have reverted to Islam and will be marrying a man from the Middle East. I have always been very easy-going and trusting, but find that I have become suspicious and jealous about my husband to be. There is no reason for my behavior but I am so afraid that he will change his mind or leave me. He always tries to reassure me that he loves me and that we will get married, but I can't seem to stop worrying. I don't understand why I've become this way.

Answer

I must first congratulate you on accepting Islam. By following the teachings of this true religion you will know that everything that happens in this world from the movement of a tiny electron to the shifting of huge galaxies in the heavens and from the external behavior of humans to the deepest unconscious thoughts in their psyche are fully determined and commanded by Allah. Accordingly, you should begin to feel that your worries about your soon to be husband leaving you are probably a symptom of your unnecessary anxiety. Any marriage whether Islamic or otherwise is a contract between a man and a woman and the possibility of breaching the contract is not totally unexpected. Let your Islamic inspiration guide you to the spiritual realm beyond this temporal world. People who are about to get married do not know whether they or their spouses may suddenly have an accident and die or that they may become physically sick or mentally disordered. Worrying about à situation can only increase one's anxiety to the point of becoming severely debilitated. Be optimistic, have trust in Allah and try to change your negative thoughts. Whenever you have an internal dialogue with yourself and get these thoughts about your future spouse leaving you, evoke within yourself positive thoughts of an optimistic and spiritual nature.

In your question you stated that you do not have a profession or work. Without a job, you are probably having a lot of time for these negative thoughts to accumulate. You can remedy this negativity by being actively engaged in some meaningful activities. You can also study and increase your knowledge about Islam. This may give you confidence and happiness. Ultimately, your mind will free itself from undue anxiety.

More about jinn possession

Question from Fatima

What is your view on someone who is possessed or 'taken over' by jinn? Is this true or is it a psychological disorder? A woman suffering from jinn possession speaks in different languages which she doesn't know, her voice becomes that of a man and she acts in a very strange manner. How should people around this person deal with her?

Answer

I already answered a similar question in the earlier part of this book. The earlier question was mainly on the possible spiritual influences that cause a possessed person to hallucinate by seeing things or hearing voices. We discussed the issue comparing it with the modern diagnosis of schizophrenia. This question relates to a different aspect. It concerns what psychologists call "altered states of consciousness". This phenomenon is puzzling to many modern Muslim psychologists and psychiatrists who are committed to their Islamic faith and way of life but who studied Western behavioral sciences that view spiritual possession with skepticism and scorn. So, in their Western psychological studies they are told that jinn or soul or any form of unobserved phenomenon of a spiritual nature should be kept outside the realm of science and should be limited to religious or metaphysical studies. Such ethereal otherworldly things, they claim, have no place in scientific psychology or psychiatry.

In answering this question I wish to inform you about the way in which different secular psychological perspectives view this issue. Behaviorists dominated the field of psychology for more than half a century and their influence is still clear in all its branches. They have not only denied the spiritual side of man but they also denied the existence of a human mind or at least they have depreciated its role in shaping human behavior. The "mind" to these extremists cannot be directly observed and thus it can only be accepted if it is used as a synonym for the brain! Psychology to behaviorists should limit itself to observable phenomena. The soul, the non-material mind and human consciousness cannot be directly observed or measured so they are not worthy of scientific study and to the extreme among them deny their very existence.

On the other platform stands Freud. He was the most influential thinker in molding modern psychology and psychiatry, and in fact, in shaping the whole of Western modernity. From a different approach, he has openly ridiculed religion and all forms of spirituality. He considered belief in God an illusion and the act of worshipping Him as an obsessional neurosis of humanity. In this secular faith, man is viewed as an animal, different from other animals only in the behavior he exhibits. His behavior should only be explained in terms of his nervous system, genes, hormones, upbringing, unconscious motivation, environment or any other variable that can be studied in their limited area. The recent cognitive revolution has curbed the extreme position of behaviorism by bringing back consciousness and its mind to psychology but it continues to support the secular philosophy of psychology. Other theories that subscribe to spiritual aspects such as that of Jung could not achieve much popularity and few psychologists follow their thought and techniques of therapy.

Thus the behavior of a person who acts as though a different being has possessed him or the one who behaves as if a number of personalities are inhabiting his body is diagnosed as suffering from a *multiple personality disorder*. This, according to their classification, is a dissociative disorder in which the afflicted person avoids his unbearable stress by 'escaping' from his personal identity. He may forget who he is or he may suddenly assume a totally different personality. When you read their intricate explanations of these phenomena in terms of unconscious sexual and aggressive conflicts and circular roundabout learning theories, you can clearly see, as a neutral observer, that to believe in the truthfulness of their claims is more demanding than to believe in jinn possession. They have a great difficulty in trying to deny any spiritual phenomena.

Western psychology and psychiatry oversimplify these spiritual phenomena by giving them special diagnostic terms. The diagnostic tag is like the handle of a suitcase. By examining the handle, you cannot know what is inside the suitcase. Similarly, by giving a secular name to a spiritual phenomenon, you have not explained what it really is! For example, it has been authenticated that some persons, after having an accident or suffering from a physical disorder suddenly find themselves talking with a foreign accent or even speaking in a foreign language that they had not studied. This phenomenon is authenticated; it cannot be denied. A famous case is that of an American woman who, after an accident started to speak Russian. Though Americans move frequently from city to city, this lady never left her hometown. She did not understand the Russian that she fluently spoke until someone who speaks the language told her what it was. Instead of investigating such cases as spiritual since the evidence is too strong to dismiss, they simply gave it a name; Foreign Accent Syndrome. As if the diagnostic tag had solved the problem.

Western psychology is thus not neutral. It is based on a new religion of secular humanism. We as Muslims should understand this very well if we wish to uphold our faith and worldview. As a WHO expert studying traditional healing in Ethiopia and Sudan in the early eighties, I have seen 'Zar' possessed persons who spoke in different languages which they do not speak in their usual life and whose voices changed and who possessed unusual psychic powers by which they could tell their clients about their personal experiences that they had kept as deep secrets.

Though such cases are few in number, some Western psychologists and medical experts are beginning to accept the influence of spiritual beings on human behavior and to agree with the therapeutic practice of exorcism. Chief among them is Scott Peck, the famous psychiatrist and author of the record-breaking book, *The Road Less Traveled.* He mentioned that he personally attended two cases of spirit possession in which the patients were cured after exorcism in a very short time in comparison to psychiatric treatment. He later wrote a book devoted to his studies on the influence of spirits. The book is titled, *Glimpses of the Devil.*

As Muslim psychologists and psychiatrists, we should not reject such spiritual influences. If patients do not respond to our psychological or drug treatment, we should not turn down the possibility of 'spiritual pathology'. In my own experience, I found that my cooperation with Muslim healers has been of great benefit to my patients, particularly those who believed that they had been spiritually influenced by evil spirits. If we want our therapy to be successful, then we should also take the patient's beliefs into consideration. If he believes in jinn possession then we should incorporate it to our healing practice.

A problem of an approach-avoidance conflict

Question from Ahmad

I am not sure if this is related to psychology but somehow I think you can help me:

I am working as a lecturer of Operations Management in one of the universities in England. The problem I have is that sometimes my intentions become a serious problem for me.

Sometimes I think inwardly with myself that what I am doing is basically teaching non-Muslims how to make more money through better organization of their work. In fact I am teaching them how to contribute more in the capitalism of the Western way of life.

As a Muslim I find this disappointing and sometimes I think of changing my field of work or going back to my original Muslim country (both of which are quite difficult). When I am in a good mood I tell myself that I am doing this job to bring "*rizq*" to my family. Therefore that should be my intention and it is good. At the same time being a good lecturer, I try to establish a good image of a Muslim for students. I then try to complete my Islamic duties by other activities as my hobbies. Sometimes I wished if I could have talked about Islam at the end of one of my lectures but as you know this is completely unacceptable in such an academic environment. This thought that I am doing something un-Islamic by teaching non-Muslims how to make their business stronger annoys me a lot. Can you advise me on what to do?

Answer

You are wondering whether your problem is psychological in nature or not. I would like to assure you that it is. At least it is a problem of a psycho-spiritual nature. First, it is a psychological problem because you are essentially suffering from an approach-avoidance conflict. You like your specialization and you seem to be a good lecturer. This is a positive approach. But you feel you are actually using your expertise to help the wrong people. This is the negative approach. When a person is enduring such a conflicting situation, even for less important issues, he can experience painful stress. If the problem is not resolved, this long lasting stress may cause him to have chronic anxiety.

Secondly, it is a spiritual problem because the conflict is caused by a religious and moral issue. That is why I am using the term "psycho-spiritual". Trying to resolve the issue by telling yourself that your job is bringing "*rizq*" to your family or that you can at times talk about Islam to your students or that your good teaching is in itself a way of indirectly preaching Islam since your students know you are a Muslim may help you in reducing the anxiety that crops up from time to time. However this would not solve the problem completely.

I can understand your problem very well because I had personally suffered from the same conflict when I was briefly teaching in the American University of Beirut during the sixties. Though most of my students were Muslims, but the American University was playing a major role in secularizing and westernizing its students and a practicing Muslim at that time might find himself a misfit. Although the years I spent as an assistant professor were among the most fruitful to me in learning new experiences in my field and in making many good friends from my Christian colleagues and old professors, I was not happy from the Islamic and spiritual standpoints. It was mainly for this reason that I accepted a lectureship appointment with a much lower salary in Omdurman Islamic University in 1968. Though I lost all my gratuity benefits by resigning from the American University without giving the proper notice, I was happy to teach in an Islamic University.

By referring to my personal experience, I do not intend to propose to you to go back to your country or to leave your job. Things are very different now from our good times in the sixties. However there are three things that you can do to help yourself in the current situation. First, in the *Sunnah* of our Prophet (ṣ) there is indeed a very great gift that helps to resolve psychological conflicts. That is *du'ā' al-Istikharah* (The prayer for choosing the better of two options). Repeat this *du'ā'* or prayer after offering a prayer of two *rak'ats*. I am sure Allah will guide you to take the right decision.

Secondly, you can apply to a university in a Muslim country such as Malaysia where your kids will not miss the good life of the west by living in an Islamic environment. At least, the vast majority of your students would be Muslims. Thirdly, since your specialization is in Business Management, you should not be a slave of the academic way of life. You may get better "*rizq*" for your family if you resign from the university teaching appointment and find a job in a commercial enterprise.

Question 18
A gifted girl mistreated by her family

Question from Waheeda

My father abused me physically and emotionally all of my life and continues to do so, I am 22 years old. I also receive overwhelming ridicule from my mother and two older male siblings. I am the scapegoat but I view them as victims to my father as well. I don't have any freedom; He does not allow me to have any friends and treats me like a child. He fully controls me. It is really bad brother. Although I have a lot to say, I cannot because there is so much to tell. I have such low self-esteem that it has led to my dismissal from college due to my poor academic performance. Although I have the ability to do very well in my studies, my lack of confidence is slowing my progress in pursuing my educational goal. I believe Allah has blessed me with a strong intellect. I will give you an example to show you how poor my self-concept is. I have been dismissed from college due to my academic performance but my parents still don't know about the dismissal because I fear what my father will do to me. I am currently attending another college to get better grades, hoping to get readmitted to my former college. I am hiding this from them and I don't know how I've done it but that's how I learned to survive in my home; to hide the things that will cause harm to me. May Allah forgive me. Please don't suggest to me to tell them the truth, because if I do, he will kill me. I wish one day I will be able to overcome this fear, but I am not ready now. Still amidst all of this, Allah has still given me a light in my heart to smile and laugh and love people, but inwardly, I suffer from this inferiority complex. I don't know how I will carry on a marriage relationship with these feelings I have about myself; *inshahAllah* I will be better by then, but how? My home environment is miserable. I sleep all day to escape everything but all that's doing is digging the hole deeper. I guess I don't know what my question to you is, brother. I want to get married but can't find a good Muslim brother and that's a problem because my father doesn't give me any freedom or trust because he is not religious himself. He wants to choose a husband for me in order to conform to our family tradition of marrying within the family or culture. He wants a rich husband with a respected family; a husband to be proud of. My mother and siblings are not helping the situation. If anything, they make me feel worse. I have a lot of sympathy for them. I forgive them without expecting an apology from them. I am sorry I am going in circles. I didn't really think out what I wanted to ask you, I guess I'm just crying out for help. My *Iman* has suffered and has never been that perfect anyway. I am looked at as the outcast and stranger since I am the religious one in the family. Islam is completely foreign to my family and most of the members of my culture. Brother Malik, advice that you give me today will make me feel better. I don't have anybody to talk to, and I don't see a way out. Please don't underestimate the gravity of my situation. In fact in my opinion, my situation is worse than you think, so when you reply to me please consider how bad it could really be because that's how bad it is. I'm sorry for being so disorganized in writing to you. I guess I'm just feeling so hopeless and need you to tell me something that I can think about or that will ease my mind for now. What I have told you is just a fraction of the enormous problems that I have.

Answer:

First I must congratulate you heartily on your ability to express yourself in such a moving and clear style. In reading your question I felt as if I am reading a novel written by a gifted writer.

Waheeda, you are a talented writer. I believe, with good practice, you can be a very good author. This confirms your belief that Allah has given you the gift of a sharp intellect.

The main advice I would like to give to you is not to be pessimistic in spite of all the negative experiences you have suffered from. From what you have written I feel that your father may be psychologically an unstable man. The way you sympathize with your brothers indicated to me that you have compassion. I would like you to develop the same feelings towards your father in spite of the harsh treatment you received from him. Look at him as somebody who is psychologically disturbed and who may be in need of your understanding and possible help. If you can muster some courage, you can speak to him in a soft and humble manner to remind him that after all you are his daughter and will continue to carry his name whether he is dead or alive. Tell him that you are ready to do the things that will please him and that you expect him to treat you with love and respect. Frequently, such parents may be touched by such an unexpected approach and some of them will genuinely change the way they treat their children.

The fact that you were free to transfer from one college to another means that you have some degree of freedom to have social contact with people outside your home. Therefore, I would advise you to look for some Muslim student groups in campus like the Muslim Student Associations if you are in North America and try to be involved in their activities. I have known of many introverted, shy, and unconfident young men and women whose life has been dramatically changed by being active members in such groups. They will meet the right people and develop a stronger spiritual attachment and motivation. It is also possible that you will meet older lecturers who can act as counselors and substitute parents to you.

If you become a devout worshipper, you will begin to see that all the harsh treatment you are receiving from your parents and siblings as a way by which Allah is raising your spiritual status in the Hereafter. If you are patient and loving to Allah, I am sure that He will very soon send you the good man who will marry you and save you from all of these problems. Hiding the fact that you have been dismissed from one college with the hope of being accepted back to the same college is fine if the possibility for re-admission is good.

One last point of optimism is that it is not difficult at all to treat people who suffer from lack of self-confidence and an inability to assert themselves. Behavior and cognitive therapist can be very helpful in this respect. You only need to find the right therapists and the time to do the therapy. If you are in North America, you can get such psychological and emotional counseling from college based counseling and social therapy programs offered on campus. However, I am sure if you become active in one of these Islamic groups, you will be cured and spiritually enhanced.

The need for a devoted worshipper as a role model

Question from Thomas Hamza

I converted to Islam a year ago, and now I am back in the United States. I don't know how to explain it, but there has been something that has mentally prevented me from praying. I am terrified from my current mental state. I feel that I am falling off of the path. How do I get on the right path? Are jinn involved here? It is difficult being a Muslim here. I have lost many friends because I do not drink anymore. Please advise me on how to overcome this predicament and renew my faith. I have definitely fallen off. Please, please help me.

Answer

I feel sad when reading about the conflicts you are experiencing. The main advice I would like to give you is to find friends who are committed Muslims and who are able to give you psychological and spiritual support. You should remember that there is a hadith by our Prophet (ṣ) that says that at the end of time the one who holds to his *Dīn* or (religion) is like the one who is holding a burning charcoal. The pleasure and reward from Allah is proportional to the difficulties that a Muslim endures in swimming against the materialistic currents of the environment in which he/she is living. Try to be conscious of Allah as he sees you and remember Him particularly when you are alone in the darkness of the night. Make passionate and sincere *Du'ā'* or supplication to Him to give you support and lead you to the right path. It is also useful for you to read book on the biography of the Prophet (ṣ) and other devoted companions and Muslim leaders regularly in order to be guided by their exemplary life. If there is a devoted Muslim worshipper in your area, then frequently visit him and ask him to pray for you. Take him as your role model. I am sure if you follow this advice you will very quickly see that the friends who urged you to drink and lead a deviant life like theirs are indeed your enemies who may lure you into addiction and venereal diseases in this life and to Divine punishment in the Hereafter.

When obsessive-compulsive disorder disturbs religious faith

Question from a Brother/Sister

I am losing myself. I have so many bad thoughts in my mind about life and Allah. I know that these are from the devil but I have become so weak to be able to prevent them. I fear I will lose myself. It seems that every day I am getting worse. I can't answer these thoughts in my mind. In the past they were accepted beliefs to me and now I am seeing and feeling evil doubts.

Answer

I have already discussed this issue in my answer to an earlier question on obsessive-compulsive neurosis. However I will discuss your problem in more detail with respect to the issue of obsessive thoughts regarding religious doubts since it seems to be a problem that afflicts many Muslims. First I would like to affirm to you that I will indeed make *du'ā'* for you, but I would like to assure you that the fact that you suffer from such an agony because of your feeling that you may be losing your faith is evidence that you are still a very good Muslim. If you were really losing your faith then you would have had no sadness or agony. People who lose their belief in God and in the unseen aspects of Islam would be happy to enjoy a new kind of life in which they would have rid themselves from the many restrictions of Islamic life. For example, they would obtain money by any means; ethically or unethically. They would enjoy forbidden sexual relations without any feelings of guilt, and would direct their ambitions and goals only to the life of this temporal world. I know a number of such people, some of them were my friends, who had been committed Muslims in their university life, and who thereafter developed doubts about their religion and eventually led a materialistic life in which they lived like secular people. They experienced no pain or agony despite losing their faith. In your case, the situation is quite different; it is the opposite. I assure you that the pain you suffer from as you hate and resist these thoughts and obsessions or *Wassawis* will indeed be a source of much reward to you from Allah. Do you think that Allah who tested you with this disorder will not reward you in the Hereafter for an agony he has inflicted over you?

The specific psychological term for this type of obsessive disorder is scrupulosity. Those afflicted would suffer from tormenting guilt, anxiety and self-devaluation regarding their religious doubts and their fear of losing their faith. The difference between them and normal people is that of cognitive and emotional responses. All people from time to time experience fleeting thoughts of such doubts and disbeliefs but they are not unduly disturbed by them since they can clearly identify them as only negative transitory thoughts triggered by their lower animalistic souls or by *shaitan* as opposed to their permanent belief in Allah and His holy messenger. They do not unreasonably blame themselves nor do they aspire for unattainable perfection. They know they are humans not angels. On the other hand, obsessive persons suffering from scrupulosity view these ugly thoughts and the emotions they create as if they were real facts. They interpret their feelings of anxiety and guilt as evidence that they have really lost their faith and doubted the truthfulness of religion.

There are a number of therapeutic procedures for this disorder. Some drugs are helpful but the more permanent treatment comes from cognitive behavior therapy. At times a combination of both may be very helpful. The patient initially takes the drug to help with the psychotherapy but once he begins to improve, he gradually stops taking the medication.

You should know that it is authenticated that some of the companions of the Prophet (ṣ) have complained to him about these fleeting ruminations of doubt. The Prophet smiled and told them that this is evidence for their good faith. Unlike other religions, Islam does not consider such inner thoughts as sinful. As the Prophet says, thoughts become sins only if one wholeheartedly accepts them, declaring his disbelief, or when he takes actions dictated by his unbelief. In another Hadith authenticated by Ahmad ibn Hanbal the Prophet is quoted to have said: "My *Ummah* (Muslims) are not held responsible for unintended mistakes or for forgetting or when they have no power to ward off an evil". The last item may obviously be related to this obsessional disorder since the disordered person cannot stop these ugly thoughts by resisting them.

Such a discourse by a Muslim therapist can be very helpful in cognitively restructuring the negative thought of the patient. He can also use mindfulness and Islamic spiritual contemplation to bring about spiritual relaxation that fights scrupulosity. So look for such a good Muslim therapist or a spiritually motivated healer.

Question 21

To shave or not to shave, that is the problem

Question from Mohamed

I am very much worried about a lady I wish to marry. She and her family have already agreed, but now, she is telling me to shave my beard! My question is how can I make her understand that having a beard is the way I wish to be?

Answer

Your problem depends on the reasons why she is asking you to shave your beard. If it is only for you to look modernized and for her to show you to her girlfriends as a handsome clean shaven young man, then I will advise you to inform her that you like yourself the way you are and that your beard is one of the religious *sunnah* of Islam and that shaving it would make you ashamed of yourself. This action is very important at this stage of your possible marriage life. It seems to me that if you submit to her request at this early stage then more unreasonable requests are bound to come.

If on the other hand, her request is related to her feelings about you and her inability to have happy future sexual relations with you because of long facial hair, then you need to reconsider this matter. If your beard is too long, you can make it shorter!

May be by becoming more familiar with her, she will no doubt be accustomed to your facial hair and love you the way you are.

Benefits and cultural harms of Western child psychology

Question Shadya

What suggestions can you give to someone who wants to study the modern psychology of child development?

Answer

The field of child development is a very important field since it helps to mold the personality of the growing child and the way he views the world. Therefore, you must be careful about what theories and practices to accept and what theories and practices to reject. You must be very critical in looking for the hidden influences of the Western materialistic philosophy in shaping these theories. In general, Western child psychological researches that are based on scientific and medical aspects such as modern studies on the physical, emotional, perceptual, and cognitive development of children should be accepted but adapted to the needs of our culture and our Islamic beliefs. However, instructions about how children should be reared and brought up should be revised according to what sort of adults we want these children to be in future. Those who formulated child psychology theories and practices in the Western world have done so in order to help their children to grow up as adults who would adjust to the Western way of life and its secular worldview. So if Muslims students of psychology read and apply material from Western texts of child development without critical judgment, they would graduate to advise Muslim parents to bring up their children with a Western mind set. Their children will grow up to be social misfits who will not live in accordance with the Islamic and cultural values of their own society.

On the other hand, we need to learn from the West how to inculcate critical and independent creative thinking in our children. We need to change our educational and instructional system that feeds unquestionable mental submission to the words of the teacher and encourages memorization and rote learning. But, at the same time we should avoid their unrestricted permissiveness that cultivates self-indulgence instead of instilling self-control and respect to parents and elders. In fact, even in the West, many educators and child psychologists are now openly blaming the advice to parents given by the early psychoanalytically oriented child psychologists and pediatricians on how to bring up their children. They hold them responsible for the moral decline and the huge increase in the rate of juvenile delinquency, rape, drug addiction and other vices that are threatening the very ethical fiber of Western nations.

Chief among those blamed for encouraging the current unrestricted permissiveness in bringing up children was the well-known pediatrician Dr. Benjamin Spock whose famous book on baby and child care first appeared in the forties of the last century. This famous book attained an unsurpassed position in printed books. Millions upon millions of copies were sold for decades to teach parents how to bring up narcissistic kids who grow up with less moral restraint and more contempt for parental authority. It became the best seller of all time.

So be analytical as a *Muslimah* in assessing Western material on child development. You will discover that whatever is supported by unbiased scientific evidence would not be in conflict with Islam as a worldview and whatever is based on the arm chair theories of secular psychologists would often be in contradiction with Islam as a way of life. Finally, I advise you to read the translation of books written by early and modern Muslim scholars on child development and rearing. For example, read the English translation of Al-Ghazali's book *Ya Ayyuha al-Walad* and the modern volumes written by Abdullah Alwan entitled *Child Rearing in Islam*.

Is masturbation a sin?
Is it physically and mentally harmful?

Question from a Brother

I am really addicted to masturbation and I do not have the means to get married. Please help me.

Answer

First and foremost I would like you to be aware of three important facts. Initially you should understand that the consensual verdict among the imams and scholars of leading theological schools and Muslim jurists is that masturbation is not a sin. It is not *ḥarām*. For example, Ahmad Ibn Hanbal the great Imam of the Hanbali School has allowed its practice, saying that the semen that a person ejaculates in masturbation is only an excess of fluid in the body similar to the blood that one loses in the blood cupping therapy. Even during the ancient blessed time of our history, a young man complained to Ibn Abbas, the learned cousin of Prophet Muhammad (ṣ) that he suffered from an irresistible sexual urge and that he massaged his private part until he ejaculates. Ibn Abbas did not tell him that it was a forbidden practice. He said it could save him from fornication.

The second issue I want you to know is that all the popularly quoted sayings of the Prophet (ṣ) that condemn masturbation and put it at the same sinful level as incest and sodomy are certainly not authenticated and most of them were fabricated; probably by parents who had wished to deter their children from overdoing it.

The third fact is that all the popular sayings about the physical and psychological harm of masturbation are not true. Masturbation, modern medicine informs us, does not lead to madness, epilepsy, or paralysis. There is no scientific evidence for such beliefs, but there is evidence that if a person continuously lives under the impression that he is committing a sin worse than incest and that his habit will end up in madness or epilepsy, he would certainly develop so much guilt and anxiety that he would come down with an anxiety or mood disorder. This unfounded guilt may even disturb his spiritual relationship with Allah.

Our young adolescent children are really living in an extremely seductive environment. Sexual abstinence in the time of Ibn Abbas in which he did not prevent masturbation cannot be compared with our extremely enticing age of pornography, voyeurism, nudity and all sorts of incitements to sex. This age of the sexual revolution cannot even be compared with our good old days of the forties of the last century. Elderly clerics who frequently choose the most extreme and harshest views on masturbation do not really appreciate the sexual agony of their children. In fact, many of them are sexually very satisfied since they are polygamous!

In supporting these views on this issue, I am not trying to encourage you to continue with the excessive practice of masturbation. That is so because if a person learns to use masturbation as a form of tension reduction and not only as a way to relieve sexual tension, he may be addicted to its excessive use. Such a person would feel the irresistible urge to masturbate whenever he feels disheartened or tense because of the normal problems of daily life.

Of course, the best remedy for you is to get married. You will definitely find a wife who is also suffering from the same kind of sexual depravation and who would accept to marry you with minimal financial and other demands. Finally, don't forget the advice of the Prophet (ṣ) to those who cannot marry. Fasting and physical exercise are helpful in reducing your sexual urge.

How to get rid of unjustified suspicion and mistrust of others

Question from Abu Safiya

My problem is that I often find myself losing confidence in my friends. I quickly become suspicious. I later feel guilty since they are Muslim companions. I tried many times to fight this but failed. Please advise me.

Answer

This feeling of unfair doubt and suspicion about other people is quite common in our modern times in which seemingly trusted persons behave in an unexpected inappropriate manner. So many people do not consider it a serious issue. Some pious Muslims would repent and pray for those whom they had wrongly accused. However, the fact that you feel guilty about this issue is a good sign that proves that you have a good heart. In more serious cases the person may have longstanding distrust and suspicion of others without feeling uncomfortable about it. Such a person strongly believes that other people are malevolent toward him and that they intend to harm, exploit or deceive him. This disorder is known in psychopathology by the term, paranoid personality disorder. It is very rare for a person who has this type

77

of personality to feel that he is wrong or to ask for therapy. A more serious paranoid disorder is seen in psychotic or mad persons whose confused mind may cause them to have irrational beliefs of suspicion and persecution.

You should thank God that your case of suspicion is a mild one. To help yourself you should reconsider whether or not you are too sensitive about the negative thoughts you develop about others or whether you are punishing yourself too much for these negative thoughts. Furthermore, I advise you to find the reason for your quick negative thought about your friends. May be in the past you have been betrayed by someone who breached your trust. May be it was so painful that you have become consciously or unconsciously on your guard not be cheated again. If so, you should convince yourself that you cannot ruin your life because of one unfortunate incident that happened in the past. Another psychological tactic is to bring into your mind the good qualities of the person whom you have unjustifiably suspected. You should train yourself to do this as soon as the thoughts of suspicion enter your mind. You should also remind yourself about your own past sins particularly those you are suspecting your friend to have committed. Tell yourself that if you had sinned against God Himself, then you should be sympathetic to others whom you think might have wronged against you. Thus, whenever you are suspicious about the behavior of a brother or sister, you must remember the unlimited mercy and forgiveness of Allah. Nobody is sure about what will happen to him in the future, and some Muslims we look down upon because of real or imagined mistake they committed may eventually be better than us in the sight of Allah. Lastly, some psychologists help their counselees get rid of unwanted thoughts by making them wear an elastic band around their wrist. Whenever the negative thoughts surface into their consciousness they immediately stretch the elastic band and let it go to painfully lash their wrist. I found this kind of aversion therapy to be useful in eliminating such negative thoughts.

Can one change his personality traits?

Question from Mofaz Sabri, Malaysia

Is it possible for a person to change his personality from an emotional disposition to a rational one and vice versa?

Answer

Many people think that the way that their personality is formed is like pouring concrete in a cast mold. Once the concrete dries up, then there is no way to change its shape. They say that just as our physical characteristics are fixed by our genes, and become our external features by which people will know who we are, our internal personality traits are also the internal fixed form by which we behave in the unique manner that people will expect from us. There is nothing further from the truth than this idea. If we can change the inherited behavior of hunting animals like dogs and falcons so that they catch the prey and refuse to eat it until the hunter comes and takes it from them, then it would be ridiculous for us to say that human personality cannot be changed. In the circus, animals are taught to change their natural instincts by dancing or by obeying their weak human trainers whom they could have easily devoured in their natural habitat.

Through learning by rewards and punishments or cognitive therapy we can gradually change the behavior of an individual and curb his emotional overreactions to provoking environmental situations. The method of choice in this respect is that used by behavioral and cognitive psychologists in treating emotionally disturbed patients who are suffering from phobias and other neurotic behaviors. More than nine centuries ago, the famous Muslim scholar Abu Hamid Al-Ghazali wrote to us in his famous book, *Ihyā' 'Ulūm al-Dīn* about how a merchant suffering from an emotional disorder characterized by uncontrollable rage outbursts was able to transform himself into a patient and amiable person. I will explain how he did it in modern terms. Before he treated himself, he used to verbally and physically attack customers and fellow merchants who provoked his anger with trivial issues. But he was a religious man, so after these attacks he would repent and have sleepless nights feeling guilty about his action. So he decided to change his 'personality'.

He paid a rude man money to curse him at home. But as the man was pouring his venomous words on him, he would force himself to relax and remember Allah repeating spiritual prayers to himself. This was repeated until he could tolerate it. Thereafter he told the man to curse him in the presence of two visitors to his house. As he felt more secure and patient, he gradually increased the number of people in front of whom he was to be cursed. In time, he asked the man to spell out his ugly words publicly in the market while he responded with a smile, relaxed in a spiritual manner. Everybody was astonished. After that he became famous for his ability to tolerate all kinds of rude people.

What were the main aspects in this therapy? There were three; first he was motivated to change, secondly he stimulated in himself with a feeling of relaxed spirituality which is opposed to anger, and thirdly he used a gradual approach in helping himself. It is only in the twentieth century that modern psychology discovered the very same approach in treating emotionally disordered patients. The one who is credited with the invention of this behavioral therapy is a psychiatrist by the name of Joseph Wolpe. He called it systematic desensitization. He followed exactly the same approach of relaxation and gradualism. Because human beings are rational beings, this behavioral treatment is now accompanied by a cognitive approach that clearly indicates to the person the irrationality of his emotionality and the rational and healthier outcome of changing. It has also been recently shown that a spiritually oriented approach in which a person can transcend the problems of everyday life and view them with a cosmological spiritual approach can make him better able to reduce the amount of emotional stress that curtails his rationality.

When you asked about the possibility of changing a person with an emotional disposition to a rational one, of course you did not mean to make a person lose his emotional disposition altogether. Without the emotions of love, anxiety, and anger life would be unbearable. What you probably meant is how to make a person less emotionally sensitive, since even to act rationally you may need some emotional support from your psychological system. However if a person is too unresponsive to situations that needs him to show some emotions, which is quite rare, one would need to help him to first act as though he were having an emotional response in such situations and to repeat this until it really becomes part of his personality. In this respect, seeing touching movies and listening to some melodious music or visiting hospitals to see terminally ill patients and sick and homeless children or listening to motivational speeches of great orators can regenerate one's spirit and warm up his cold emotional state.

A blessed struggle against doubt

Question from Hawwa

I am struggling not to lose hope and faith in Allah – *"Iman"*.

Answer

Your brief statement tells me that you are really making a lot of psychological and spiritual effort to keep your faith intact. I must congratulate you on this effort because without really being a good *Muslimah* you will not struggle to uphold your *Iman*. If you were a person who does not care about whether she believes and submits to Allah or not, you would not have gone through the agony and stress of fighting to keep your *Iman*. Please do not allow *shaitan* or pessimistic thoughts undermine your belief in the mercy of Allah. Although you may not know this, this struggle that you are going through may result in much reward from Allah. My dear daughter Hawwa, we are living in a very bad time. This is the end of time in which everything around us entices us to enjoy whatever is *ḥarām* and to find aversion to whatever is *halal*. It is the time of the dominant secular culture with its influential media. For this reason the Prophet (ṣ) gave good tidings to Muslims of later ages like us who struggle to keep their *Iman*. He described this situation by saying that a time would come when a person who upholds his religion would be like a person who is holding a burning charcoal in his hand. He said that those who succeed in resisting temptation and the evil promptings of both humans and evil spirits would be given a reward that is ten times the reward given to those who lived during the Prophet's time and performed the same deeds.

So I would like you to be optimistic. Allah will not leave you alone because He is merciful and loving and responds abundantly to any minor step that a Muslim takes towards receiving His mercy. I hope my dear daughter Hawwa that you are not living in a depressing environment that causes you so much stress that leads you to have negative feelings towards your relationship with Allah. If there is any truth in this statement, then you should not confuse your problems with the reality of faith. And if your environment is in some ways causing you to have this problem, then try to change to another one if you can. Finally, I advise you to find a good Muslim friend or counselor who can help you overcome your spiritual difficulties.

All Muslims, including the companions of the Prophet (ṣ), used to get transient bad thoughts concerning their Islamic faith. This is what is referred to as *waswas*. When normal Muslims get these fleeting ugly thoughts of *kufr*, they take refuge in Allah and curse *shaitan* who has forced them into their hearts and consciousness. Read the last surah of the Holy Qur'an *"Al-Nās"* and contemplate about its meaning. However if these thoughts are seriously dominating your consciousness, it may be a form of obsession. In this case, it would be the psychological disorder of obsessive-compulsive disorder (OCD). If it is that then read what I have previously written about the distress that OCD can cause to one's religious belief.

Question 27
Finding difficulty in performing prayers

Question from Amr, UK

As a Muslim I am aware of my responsibilities to my creator and have tried to follow them all to the best of my ability. I have, *Alhamdulillah,* done Ḥajj and *Umrah* and I fast every Ramadan and I am worried about the current tragic events that are taking place in the *Ummah.* However I have great difficulty in performing the 5 daily prayers every day. I have to admit that sometimes I can spend days without praying. I become very lazy and feel prayer is burdensome. I feel very guilty because I am conscious of my shortcoming. The problem is that I work shifts so I do not have a consistent daily life pattern. What can I do to improve this situation? Please advise me. My guilt intensifies when I remember that I have children whom I want to bring up as good Muslims.

Answer

It was found that many people like you whose jobs require them to alternate their work schedule between day and night develop serious stress and some of them may come down with depression. I wonder whether your feelings of laziness, retardation and guilt are not in reality symptoms of a mild depression. It may be a good idea to see a Muslim counselor to discuss this issue with him or her. The fact that you have performed Ḥajj and *Umrah* shows that you are a committed and dedicated Muslim. But if after that you find prayer to be a heavy burden is not considered normal behavior. I would suggest to you to look for dedicated Muslim friends with whom you can at times perform congressional prayers, *Jama'a* and discuss Islamic issues and listen to some religious songs. What you really need is some spiritual inspiration. Such a good friend can also make your life happier and more interesting.

It would also be useful if you can make a schedule of your daily activities that would raise your morale such as regular physical exercise, reading Islamic literature and attending religious motivational lectures that are spiritually enhancing by Muslim scholars in your area. If you return from your work tired and you simply lie down in bed doing nothing other than contemplating on the dark side of your life, you may gradually slip into a more serious depressive mood. Get rid of laziness and idleness and develop an optimistic attitude in your life.

Question 28

An unresolved conflict between having a second wife and being deprived from having children

Question from Zaid

I understand that the nature of my problem is complicated. We are happily married and try to follow Islam as a way of life as far as we can. My wife had a very serious female disease, due to which the doctor had to remove her uterus completely. We lost all hope of having kids. We took everything as a test from Allah. For the last two years I started to become depressed. I am now unable to do well in my research job. I consulted a psychiatrist and a psychologist and they gave their medical treatment and psychological advises, however I am not back to my normal self. My wife, who is really an extraordinarily good woman, suggested to me to take a second wife but not to divorce her. I love her so much and I will never think of divorcing her. But according to USA legal system, as far as I know, I cannot marry a woman as long as I have a wife. My wife wholeheartedly wants me to marry another woman but I cannot do that according to USA legal system. This is a serious crime. My request to you is to provide me with an Islamic solution to our problems and according to USA legal system. I will deeply appreciate your kind advice that can be applicable to the legal injunctions of USA. Please give me good cyber-counseling.

Answer

Your case reminds me of a similar problem faced by an Indonesian brother living in Germany. This was back in the early eighties when I visited his city to give a talk to the Indonesian Islamic Society. He was the leader of the group and was one of the most spiritually motivated people I have met in my life. Whenever he is in a dilemma, he would make *Salat Al-Istikharah* to pray to Allah to choose the better alternative for him. More often than not he would see the Prophet (ṣ) himself in a dream that would tell him what to do. One early morning, a middle-aged committed German Muslim lady came to their headquarters saying that she had a daughter who was 18 years old at the time and who was extremely beautiful. The mother wanted one of the young Indonesian men to marry her daughter in order to save her from the temptations of the material life of Germany.

When this mother became a Muslim she divorced her Christian husband and lived in a German Turkish community. The mother was happy to wear the Hijab, but the daughter started to revolt against her mother reminding her that she too had come to Islam after living freely as a German woman and that she too wanted to experience the same kind of materialistic life before coming to the traditional Islamic way of life. The mother wanted her to get married to a good Muslim who will be able to change her thoughts. The Indonesian brothers asked their leader to marry this young lady. The Indonesian brother told me that he made the *Istikharah* prayers but an unexpected dream would reoccur to him again and again. Whenever he tried to hold the hand of the girl, he would find himself holding and embracing her mother.

He was finally convinced that he was to marry the mother

and not the daughter. The mother was at least 15 years older than him and like your wife she had undergone a hysterectomy and could not give him any children. When he told her about the dream and asked her hand, she asked for a few weeks of retreat where she can also make *Istikharah* prayers. She finally accepted but informed him that she would be very happy to take care of his children when he marries a second wife. The brother told me that he loved this woman so much after marriage that he never thought of taking another wife and that he never feel sorry about not having children. He later realized that the daughter was so enticed by the glittering life of the youth in Germany that all his efforts as husband of her mother to save her from the corrupt life she chose for herself totally failed.

In your case brother Zaid, you can have another wife and get children without filing an official declaration of marriage. I have no knowledge about the American legal system but I know that in the State of Utah in western USA, the Mormons are polygamous. I read that one psychologist living in that state decided to move to another city in the US. When he left, 20 women followed him! You can investigate about how they get away with it and do the same thing. However if you decide not to take another wife, you can opt for 'adopting' a child. In Islam, the Western law that requires you to give your name to the adopted child is prohibited because Islam guards against creating confusion regarding lineage. But bringing up an orphan is one of the best deeds in Islam. The wisdom of Islam in this ruling is quite obvious. In many countries that follow the Western laws of adoption much psychological harm may be done to the adopted children. They would discover after a number of years that their adoptive parents are not their real biological parents. Many of them become extremely disappointed in being cheated. Some of them will not trust their adoptive parents anymore and they may become psychologically disordered. But if the child knows at an early age that his adoptive parents are not his or her biological parents he or she would accept and have a normal happy childhood. That is so because their adoptive parents would love them in the same way they would love their own biological children. I have known a number of such cases in Sudan in which children brought up in such homes care for their guardians in old age in a way which I would have doubted whether their own biological children would have done.

My dear Zaid, if you love your wife to the extent that you hesitate to harm her feelings by taking another wife, then you should seriously think about being a guardian to a Muslim orphaned child. In this way, you can save a Muslim child from being adopted by a non-Muslim family where he or she may lose their identity. You must be aware of the hadith in which the Prophet (ṣ) said: "I and the guardian of an orphan in paradise are like this" pointing to his middle and index finger and slightly separated them; meaning that these guardians will have a very close status to that of the Prophet (ṣ) in paradise. The editor of this cyber-counseling program emailed me just now to inform you that there is a refugee Iraqi Muslim community somewhere in California that has children for adoption.

However if you decide to take another wife, I advise you not to choose a younger and more beautiful wife than your present wife. Many women may be happy to allow their husbands to take a second wife but if he brings a younger and more beautiful wife they may become extremely jealous. Another important issue you need to deal with is that of your property. You need to ask a Muslim cleric as to whether you should give your wife now a good share of your money and property before getting your second wife. It may be unfair to her to reach her old age without children while most of your money and property may go to your children.

A shy wife who cannot comply with her husband's sexual request

Question from a Sister

I love my husband very much but he likes me to say sexual words to him during our sexual intercourse but I feel too shy and embarrassed to do so. How can I please him?

I am too shy to mention my name!

Answer

I wondered whether to publicly write my answer to your embarrassing question or to confidentially send it to your email through the interviewer. I decided to write it publicly since it can be a useful advice to many women who find the sexual requests of their husbands embarrassing. We live in a morally challenging age of sexual enticement. It is the age of pornography and the AIDS pandemic. To help young people we find ourselves forced to speak about issues that were taboo only a few years ago.

Many husbands often come to their wives with strange sexual demands. I believe that it is advisable for women to accept doing such requests. When they refuse, some husbands may seek to satisfy these fantasies elsewhere. So, in answering your question I first wish to draw your attention to this simple phenomenon. Women in general would not feel shy to expose all of their bodies to their husbands during sexual intercourse but feel shy to undress when changing their clothes in front of them in the absence of sexual stimulation. The inability or extreme shyness to vocalize obscene words is a similar learnt behavior. These are related to childhood experiences in which undressing in front of others or saying sexually explicit words had been harshly prevented by parents and had been associated with shamelessness. What causes embarrassment and shyness is not the sexual meaning of the words as much as the association of pronouncing these colloquial informal words that had been conditioned with shameless and immoral behavior. Thus saying words that carry the same meaning in classical or foreign language would cause little or no embarrassment. A male gynecologist told me that Arab women are generally terribly ashamed to describe their symptoms to me. But if they shift to speaking in English, they can go into detailed descriptions without much embarrassment. It is clear here that it is not the meanings but the actual tabooed words.

So, women can make their husbands sexually happier if they cooperate in satisfying their idiosyncratic sexual fantasies however they should avoid the two practices that are prohibited by Islam. These are anal sex and penetrative vaginal sex during the monthly menstruation of the wife. All other practices, which satisfy the husband or the wife, are permissible. In many cultures, women are trained by their female elders to respond with verbal sounds and words to please their husbands during sexual intercourse. If you feel that some of these sounds and words embarrass you, try to train yourself to repeat them again and again during the day until you disrupt their connection with your learnt shyness response. After that, you can utter them without so much embarrassment. As I mentioned, it is possible that you were rebuked by your parents when you uttered them as a child and extreme shyness became a fixed conditioned response. You can start by uttering the least embarrassing words and gradually please your husband with more provoking ones.

Question 30
Extremism verses moderation in worshipping

Question from Halima

I am very worried about my husband. He has gone very deep into Islam in a very short time and he has lost interest in everything. He barely eats a meal a day. He is not working and is not motivated to find a job. He is spending all his money on Islamic books and computer software and I am helplessly watching him unable to do anything. I would appreciate any advice you can give me to help me deal with this situation.

Answer

The symptoms you have described are quite common among those who have the tendency to be too extreme in their interpretation and practice of religion. This kind of religious extremism had been noticed very early by a female companion of Prophet Muhammad (ṣ). She came to visit the Prophet's wife Aisha who observed that the woman appeared disheveled and not caring for her grooming. When Aisha asked her why she was so careless about her physical appearance, she answered by saying that her husband has become so zealous in his religious practices to the extent that he lost interest in all material aspects of life. He was continually fasting and worshiping. Furthermore, he lost interest in women. Aisha told the Prophet (ṣ) about the agony of this lady. The Prophet (ṣ) immediately called the husband and said to him, "Have I not been informed that you fast all the day and stand praying all night?" The husband answered, "Yes O Messenger of Allah" The Prophet (ṣ) then said, "Do not do that all the time. Fast for a few days and also do not fast in other days; stand for night prayers some nights and sleep in others. Your body has a right over you ... and your wife has a right over you". The husband complied with the Prophet's (ṣ) advice and adopted a moderate Islamic approach. After that, Aisha (may Allah be pleased with her) was happy to see his wife well dressed and attractive.

In my own experience I have seen such brothers who become so extreme because of their previous deviant life. Some of them were communists who openly declared their atheism and others were slaves to their material desires. After radically changing from a materialistic or immoral way of life to an Islamic worldview in which they become inspired by the beauty of spiritualism, they experience much guilt for what they had done in the past. To atone, they change from one extreme to other. They fail to lead a balanced Islamic life. A third group of religious extremists are those who suffer from some forms of personality disorders before becoming Muslim activists. These are the ones who would have displayed such kind of extremism had they joined any group whether it were Islamic or not.

Sister Halima, I am not quite sure in which category your husband would be diagnosed. It is my ardent hope that he would be like the companion of the Prophet (ṣ) whose main aim in life was to please Allah. Such highly devoted Muslims can easily be brought back to Islamic moderation when they realize that the pleasure of Allah can only be fully secured by such moderation. I am sure you have heard about the hadith of the Prophet (ṣ) in which he rebuked three of his companions because one of them claimed that he stopped any sexual relations with women, the second one decided to fast every day of his life except those days in which fasting is prohibited by *Shariah*, and the third person went to the extreme of praying and worshiping throughout the night without sleeping. The Prophet called them and angrily reprimanded them for their excessive behavior by stating that: Surly I am the most God fearing among you yet I have marital relationships, I don't fast every day of my life, and I worship at night and sleep as well. He concluded by stating a solemn verdict, "This style of life or *sunnah* is my way, so the one who do not follow my *sunnah* is not one of us". I hope if your husband can read this and can consult those who are knowledgeable to guide him to the right Islamic path. I also advise you to look for clerics or friends or older relatives whom he respects to help him resolve this dilemma.

Unwarranted feeling of inferiority because of dark skin color

Question from a Muslimah

I actually submitted my question a few times. Last time when I submitted this problem to you, you told me to check in the archives. I did but the answer has not been posted due to technical errors. I'm sorry to disturb you again with having you to answer the question, which I think you remember, but I will repeat it again. My question is about being a dark-skinned woman married to a light-skinned man and all the cultural stereotypes and prejudices that come with this situation. Generally, I have always had a good amount of self-confidence, but after I was married, and not through my kind husband's actions, I do feel inferior because of my color, especially when I am around people who consider dark skin as something weird. In such situations, my self-esteem becomes considerably low. Sometimes I don't care about this issue, and at other times I just feel like I am quite unattractive to my husband. This causes me to feel distant and unloving to him. Occasionally I get extremely jealous when my self-esteem is low. *Alhamdulillah*, this issue is becoming less important. However, I wish I can get over it. I do turn to Allah and thank Him for what He has given me, and I appreciate the company of practicing Muslims to whom this issue doesn't matter. But my greatest concern is I can stop being oversensitive about how people see me because of my dark skin. I do not like to have feelings of being

unattractive to my kind husband.

Answer

I think I have answered this question before. May be it was deleted by mistake. I shall now repeat what I said for your sake. I am happy to know this feeling of inferiority regarding you complexion is becoming less frequent and I am sure with time you will get over this trivial issue once and for all. Your case reminds me of a white American brother. He is a practicing counselor who was able to successfully blend his academic specialization with Islam. This brother, though white, has always preferred dark skinned women. His first wife, an African American, reverted to Islam. At first, he was distressed with her conversion but he was impressed by her acquired spirituality and virtuous character. This helped him see the light and to convert to Islam as well. He loved her very much and saw her as the person who guided him to the right path. After a few years the wife died at a young age. He married another African American woman. This wife is a very committed Muslimah who told him that she does not want any monetary dowry from him aside from taking her to Hajj. I visited this brother in his house in the 1980's and really felt that his marriage was an ideal one.

My daughter I feel that this whole issue of inferiority regarding your complexion is probably only in your mind. Once you begin to think in this manner, then every whisper and gossip between any female guests in your house will give you the wrong impression that they may be talking about you or alluding to the difference in complexion between you and your husband. "Iblis" will use this opportunity to make you unhappy with the way God created you. I know one sister who had a fair skin but she developed leprosy and she had colorless patches in the skin of her face and hands. In spite of this, she continued to perform her obligatory Islamic duties without feelings of shame or anger about Allah's fate for her. Since in your previous letter you said that you are an attractive woman, you should be happy with what you have and forget about other illusions. I would like to conclude this answer, by telling you that in the Sudan, my own country, people in general do not like very fair women. Many of them prefer women with dark color. And when I first came to Malaysia, I told my Malay wife who is a fair woman that I find dark Indian women attractive. She told me that before I mentioned this to her, she did not appreciate this attractive aspect of Tamil Indians of Malaysia, but after that she was able to see them for the beauty that they have. I am sure the good words that your husband is saying to you are not only to raise your morale. He may be sharing with me the same opinion of appreciating the beauty of dark women. May be that is why he asked your hand in the first place.

Indecisiveness concerning marriage

Question from Sister 'S', Canada

Alhamdulilah, I will soon be getting married to a man from the Middle East. I was born and raised in Canada, and reverted to Islam as an adult. I was previously married and have a child from that marriage who was not raised in an Islamic environment. Lately, I have been suffering from anxiety thinking about how she will adjust to her new situation. Sometimes, I even want to delay the wedding, just to give myself more time to deal with this. My future husband is supportive, but I worry that he may not have been realistic in considering how difficult it may be for my daughter. We have discussed it in great detail, but I still can't stop worrying. I have been unable to sleep and am making myself ill over this.

Answer

First I would like to congratulate you on accepting Islam as a religion and way of life. Also I would like to congratulate you for finding a good Muslim husband. I think the best way for you is to make the Islamic decision-making prayer *"Istikharah"*. You can ask one of the knowledgeable brothers or sisters to teach you how to do it. After you have performed this prayer and sincerely asked Allah to guide you to do what is best for you in this world and in the hereafter, you should put your trust in Him and take the course that you feel is good for you.

You did not mention to me the age of your daughter since this factor may influence the course you should take. However, as a *Muslimah*, you have the right to satisfy your emotional and physical needs as a woman. If you are certain that your future husband is a man of compassion and patience in a way that would make him gradually win the respect and liking of your daughter, then go ahead with the marriage. I would also like you to compare the possibility of your life as a single *Muslimah* trying to bring up your daughter in an ideal Islamic way free from the materialistic life of Canada by living with a Muslim husband who can give your daughter a good example of a peaceful and loving family. The fact that you are anxious and unable to sleep is a clear indication that this approach-avoidance conflict is already affecting you psychologically. The more you continue without taking a decision the more will your anxiety increase. You have rights as a *Muslimah* and should not feel guilty about getting married unless you feel sure that your future husband is a selfish person who would create problems for you and your daughter. But if, on the contrary, you feel that he is a good man then go ahead and marry him. Islam is not like Catholicism, if things do not go in the way you expect, you can always ask him for a divorce. Also, in an Islamic marriage, the husband can give the wife the right to divorce. You can ask him to give you this right to help you to get rid of your apprehension and hesitation.

Are personality disorders a psychopathology or bad and selfish behavior?

Question from a Muslimah from Malaysia

How does one determine if someone has a borderline personality disorder or this person is just following his desires? Are personality disorders mental illnesses or are they a result of people not following Allah's commands?

Answer

The area of personality disorders and that of sociopathy and psychopathy are areas that are not clearly demarcated in abnormal and clinical psychology. Though they are not considered as psychotic or mental disorders they are looked at as disorders that are very difficult to treat. Some psychiatrists believe that some of these disorders are untreatable. Some theories propagate that they are biologically determined and accordingly they cannot be treated with psychotherapeutic intervention. However, these views are greatly influenced by the fact that modern psychiatry has neglected the moral concept of evil in human behavior thereby downgrading human responsibility. Behaviors that were considered immoral and sinful actions of yesterday are today secularized and watered down to become pathological behaviors influenced by early childhood upbringing, environmental conditions or biological etiologies. Furthermore, modern psychology and psychiatry denies the spiritual dimension in helping people with such disorders. So, they have readily accepted the biological and inherited predisposition in causing personality disorders. This supposed biological explanation is useful in saving psychologists from admitting their failure in treating such persons.

However, the experiences of many people who were thought to have suffered from untreatable or very difficult to treat personality disorders such as the so called borderline personality disorder and who have eventually undergone a spiritual conversion have quickly improved. This clearly disconfirmed psychiatry's tag of untreatable developmental or biological diagnoses. I knew a few persons whose 'disorder' fitted neatly into the symptomatology of borderline personality disorder such as hostility, impulsivity and extreme change of mood who became well-mannered citizens after they had a religious or spiritual conversion such as being influenced by Sufi healers. The most convincing evidence in this respect came from the movement of the Black Muslims of America. Many imprisoned African Americans who had been diagnosed as psychopaths, delinquents, hardened criminals, and personality disordered diametrically changed into peaceful spiritually inspired persons after they inverted to Islam. Several heroine and alcohol abusers among them were helped by their previously addicted Muslim brothers. They achieved sobriety. During the last century, a number of professionals who studied this phenomenal change in black Muslims urged psychologists to study it in order to reformulate these psychiatric labels.

So I believe my sister that many of the so called personality disordered people who go against the teachings of their religion and their cultural ethical mores in order to immediately satisfy their selfish desires should not only be considered as psychiatric patients but also as selfish persons who cannot resist the temptation of immediate gratification of their hedonistic lifestyle.

Question 34
The problems of cross-cultural marriages

Question from Iman

Salam I am having serious doubts about whether I and my husband are compatible. I am feeling really frustrated with the way in which our marriage is going as he wants me to curb and restrict the way in which I speak and react to him. When I try to address him when I have a problem with the way he treats me he says that this is the way he is and he is not going to change. I am American and he is African so there is a clash of cultures in the way in which he is accustomed to communicate with women. I feel I am making all the sacrifices and concessions for what he wants yet he feels that I have done nothing since this is what is expected from me. This has really affected all aspects of our marriage. I know he has a strong faith in Allah and I respect him for that but I don't feel our relationship is healthy and I don't feel good about myself when I am around him. Since we have been together I find myself much more emotional and depressed and feel that it may be best to part ways.

Answer

Your problem is not a unique or isolated one. I know of many cross-cultural marriages in which the spouses find themselves in a dilemma of cultural conflict. It seems to me that you are a convert to Islam and that you have lived your earlier life in a liberal way. On the other hand your husband might have been brought up in an environment in which some of the Islamic teachings about the respect of the wife to her husband has been misinterpreted and confused with indigenous customs in which woman are treated like obedient servants.

I had a number of cases in my family therapy in which the wife who is a convert to Islam but she cannot totally rid herself from some of her earlier liberal customs that are not compatible with Islam or with that of the Arab, African or Asian cultures. Moreover, modern Muslim husbands fail to see the difference between the teachings of Islam and the traditions of their native cultures. Most of them expect the wife to be an obedient maid, cooking, washing clothes, cleaning the house, taking care of the kids and sexually active at night. It may be of interest to you to know that Islam does not make it an obligation on the wife to cook and wash her husband's clothes, or do the house work. If she does, she should be thanked and appreciated.

Prophet Muhammad (s) used to help his wives with their home chores. Umar ibn Al-Khatab, the second *khalifah* used to publicly appreciate his wife's help for preparing his food and washing his clothes. He looked at it as a charity. Not only that, but Islam does not make it an obligation on the wife to nurse her baby if there is a problem between her and her husband that may end in divorce. In this case, the Holy Qur'an clearly tells the husband, to pay his wife for nursing her baby. If she refuses to breast feed her own baby then the husband needs to find another woman to nurse the infant.

If this is the case, then husbands who are brought up in traditional Muslim cultures should be advised to practice their religion in its purist form and maintain an ideal matrimonial relationship that is free from un-Islamic cultural beliefs. A few weeks ago, I counseled a couple who came to me with a problem similar to yours. The husband is an Asian and the wife a European convert. After discussing the importance of understanding and respecting the differences in their cultural norms, I spoke to the husband alone. I told him that he should develop the capability to appreciate his wife. I told him that his wife has left her own people to come and live in his country, she left her religion to come to his religion, and she left her home and family to come and stay with him. I said, "What will happen to you if you were to offer such sacrifices and they are not appreciated?" I also warned him, that if he antagonizes his wife until she develops a negative attitude to Islam, then he would bear responsibility for that in the Day of Judgement. From the way he contemplated on what I said and the way his face changed, I felt that he has realized what his wife had done for him and the agony she was suffering from. They did not come to see me again!

My dear daughter Iman, I would suggest to you to consider your husband as a person who is undergoing a conflict between submitting to his traditions which make it difficult for him to be gentle and humble with women and the liberal moral values of Western civilization where women are allowed to fight for their rights. It is sad to say that most of these rights were really what Islam preached to the harsh and crude Arab Bedouins of Arabia. Accordingly, I would like you to treat him as though you were a counselor who is helping her counselee to get over such a conflict. If you display this gentleness and understanding, and ask him to take Prophet Muhammad (ṣ) as his role model, it may eventually change his behavior. You may also seek the help of some of his friends or those whom he respects in the community to advise him without showing that you had told them.

If all these efforts fail and you feel that you cannot cope, then parting may be the bitter solution. However, I must tell you that I have been counseling many women who said they could not tolerate their husbands and were accordingly given a divorce but they later found life without their ex-husbands much more unbearable. So I advise you if you decide to get a divorce from your husband, you should sincerely ask God to choose what is best for you.

A young man who wishes to know where he can study for a M.A. degree

Question from Aziz

First of all I wish to have your email address to discuss a number of issues. Secondly, I have a problem concerning my inability to decide where I should study for my M.A. I got my B.A. from Al-Azhar University in Cairo, but I want to study for my postgraduate in Islamic Law in the International Islamic University in Malaysia. My problem is that I am not very good in Arabic so it will be difficult for me to study in Egypt. I am also not quite good in English so the Islamic university in Malaysia will require all students who apply for admission to have a high English proficiency.

Please advise me.

Answer

If you want to specialize in *Sharī'ah* and Islamic Studies then being proficient in the Arabic language is a prerequisite. If you study for your Masters in Malaysia, you will not be able to be proficient in Arabic at a level which will make you a distinguished scholar in Islamic studies in the Arab world. Accordingly, I suggest that you register for your M.A. in Egypt and make an effort to improve your Arabic to an advanced level. After obtaining your M.A. and high level of proficiency in Arabic, you can join the International Islamic University in Malaysia to do your Ph.D. Six months should be enough to improve your English to the level that would make you understand all courses taught in English at the university. So use the chance of your temporary stay in Cairo to be proficient in Arabic.

Question 36

The need to change one's conception about the nature of Allah

Question from a Brother/Sister

I am feeling depressed and sinful. I feel that an extremely terrible thing is waiting for me. It is as if I have read my future. I want to change that. The only thing that gives me some hope and peace is the verse of the Qur'an that says, "There is nothing for one except for that which he strives for". It gives me hope that one can change his ill fate. I don't know what to think. I feel that God has abandoned me and my family members. I sometimes get feelings about committing suicide. Please help me and support me with quotations that give me hope.

Answer

By being so pessimistic and despondent, you are probably committing a much greater sin than the sins that might have made you feel so bad about yourself. A Muslim should always be optimistic about his or her future. Whatever happened in the past will be forgiven by Allah. Allah simply wants you to humbly ask for His forgiveness. You must be sincere and repentant. But if your determination weakens and you find yourself repeating the same wrongdoing, you will find the door of God's forgiveness and mercy widely open.

Allah has honored humans with a soul. This soul does not

belong to us and we do not have the right to humiliate or punish it with the whip of pessimism and guilt. The prophet (ṣ) says that a Muslim does not have the right to humiliate himself. He also said that: "Anyone who pronounces the belief that '*There is no god except Allah*', enters paradise". Another very important hadith of the prophet (ṣ) related to your condition is his famous saying: "Seek optimism and you will find it".

As I mentioned to you, excessive pessimism that leads to despair from the mercy of Allah in this world and the hereafter is one of the greatest sins that a person can commit since it is based on a negative conception of Allah as unmerciful and un-forgiving. In "Surah Yusuf" in the Qur'an, Allah tells us about the Prophet Ya'qoub or "Jacob" who lost his dearest son Yusuf and was not sure whether his son was dead or alive. Yet he told his other elder sons to go and look for him and not to despair from the help and spiritual support of Allah because it is only the unbelievers who despair from divine grace. And indeed his prayers were answered and he found his beloved son, Yusuf. These verses from the Qur'an clearly point to us that seeing the world with extreme pessimism and hopelessness is not an attribute of a good Muslim. Allah has chosen you to be a believer in Him; to be a Muslim. Out of the billions on earth who do not know who Allah is. He gave you a heart that fears Him and submits to Him and loves Him. What more do you want!?

It is of interest to note that the whole field of modern cognitive psychology stresses the fact that our negative gloomy thoughts are the ones responsible for the pessimistic and depressing feelings that can psychologically cripple us. Cognitive therapists do in their clinics today, teach depressed and anxious patients to challenge their negative thoughts and change them with optimistic and positive ones. Patients who are treated by these methods quickly recover from their depressed mood. Accordingly, if you objectively challenge the thoughts that make you expect a dark future and bad fate you will be able to conquer them since more often than not they are based on unsound premises and irrational conclusions.

It seems to me that you come from a traditional Muslim family. In these families children are brought up to imagine and think of Allah only as a punishing and retributive God. Parents would always use this myopic concept of Allah to threaten their children and prevent them from doing whatever they don't want them to do. The image of Allah as the loving, merciful, compassionate Creator is neglected in bringing up these miserable children. That is why they grow up to be depressed or aggressively join extremist and militant groups. If this is the case with you, then you should read the literature on the loving, compassionate, and merciful attributes of Allah. It is quoted that the prophet (ṣ) was once sitting and having a conversation with his companions when they saw a woman frantically looking for her lost toddler. When she found him she strongly embraced him tearfully expressing tremendous emotions of joy and love for finding him. This sight was quite moving to the companions. Prophet Muhammad (ṣ), seeing the passionate feelings in their faces, said, "Are you moved and amazed by the love of this mother to her son? I vow to you that Allah is more loving and merciful to his slaves than this woman to her son".

So my dear son or daughter, I strongly advise you to change your conception about Allah. Do not allow these pessimistic dark thoughts to drive you away from the righteous path of Allah and don't let Iblis (shaitan) tell you that there is no hope in the future and incite you to commit the most abominable sin of taking your own life. I also advise you not to stay alone ruminating about these ugly thoughts. Try to find good Muslim friends to associate with and to seek their help in changing your negative thoughts and feelings. Make *du'ā'* to Allah from the bottom of your heart to alleviate these un-Islamic symptoms and to grant you a good blessed conclusion to your life.

If in spite of all these proposals you find yourself unable to see hope and redemption because of your pessimism, then you have to see a psychiatrist. You may be suffering from depression. Extreme pessimism and feeling of guilt are among its main symptoms. However it can be helped by psychiatric and psychological treatment in a short time.

A problem caused by a religious conversion

Question from a Muslim from the US

My wife and I met and we became involved when she was not a practicing Muslim and I was a Christian. However, I spent time overseas and learned about Islam. I soon embraced the religion and *Alhamdulillah*, I took the *shahadah*. Now, my love for Islam and my faith in Allah has become stronger but my wife is pretty much still the same. I find us growing apart more and more. I pray alone in my home when she is watching TV in another room. We now have a son and my problem is becoming more acute because I want him to grow up in an Islamic environment. We don't have relations with each other anymore but there is no animosity. I love her but I find myself somewhat sacrificing my religion for the sake of the marriage. I find that dangerous. Any advice would be appreciated.

Answer

Your case is not uncommon. I know of a number of brothers and sisters who were Christians who fell in love with Muslim women and men. They later studied Islam and reverted. In all of these cases the spouses were not practicing Muslims. In most cases, the Muslim wife would tell the Christian young man that my parents will not allow me to marry a Christian. So please say you have converted only for us to tie the knot! The Christian husband that 'converted' only on paper, will reverts to Islam in reality. Some of them become devoted and committed Muslims. After this conversion, he would ask his Muslim wife to dress modestly, not to drink alcohol, and not to go to mixed parties. In most of the cases that I know, the wife would refuse to comply with the husband's demands in spite of being a born Muslim. A number of these brothers had to divorce their wives and marry women who were committed to their religion; women who would share their spiritual aspirations and give them marital happiness. In a few instances, it was the Christian wife who reverted. In a case that I know very well, the woman thanked the husband for introducing her to Islam. She was patient and treated him so nicely that he finally came back to practice the religion that he was born into!

In your case, I advise you to speak to your wife in a gentle manner that does not arouse her anger and express your gratitude to her for having led you to Islam. Make her feel ashamed of herself for leading you into her own religion and failing to comply with its teachings. Make her feel that this is a serious issue and without changing her ways, life with her will become a heavy spiritual burden on you. Give her some time to change. If she doesn't then let her feel that you may end up marrying another committed Muslim woman. If even after that she refuses to change, then you should seriously think seriously about divorcing her. You are still young and you can have a happy Muslim home for your son.

Some Muslim scholars may tell you that a Muslim is allowed to live with a Christian wife and that your wife, though not a practicing Muslim, she is at least a *Muslimah* and that you should tolerate living with her. This kind of advice can be of help to a person who is living in a Muslim environment where the child will grow up with devoted Muslim uncles, aunties, cousins and teachers around him. But in our age and in your region, everything around your son would not encourage him to be a good Muslim. So he really needs a committed mother to help him live as a devoted Muslim in a secular materialistic society. You also need to share moments of happiness with a spiritually motivated companion.

If your wife does not change eventually, you will, in future, become an alienated elderly man and you may repent for not having married when you were young. Though I sincerely gave you the advice that my profession as Muslim counselor would require me to, I would still advise you to re-submit your question to another Muslim scholar for further confirmation.

A case of a mono-symptomatic phobic anxiety that is only related to speaking in public

Question from a Brother

How can I improve my confidence in myself? I don't know why exactly but every time I need to speak in front of people, my heart starts to beat very fast; may be 130 beats per minute. In general I am not someone who has a low esteem. I am educated and I feel good about myself. But this self-esteem evaporates in some stressful social situations. It seems to get out of hand especially in giving lessons and reading Qur'an. Do you have some tips in order to counteract this problem?

Answer

I already discussed this issue in a previous question. The item is titled, "Lack of confidence and social anxiety" but because of the importance and repeated questions on this issue, I shall repeat my answer from a different perspective. This problem can happen to some people after a traumatic experience in which they become very anxious while talking or socializing with others. The treatment of this social phobia is very promising. Psychologists apply what is known as systematic desensitization, which is based on special techniques of behavior modification. The process is very simple. It consists of inducing the counselee to become serene and relaxed while asking him to imagine himself engaging in gradually more demanding social situations. The process of relaxation is brought about by taking mild tranquilizers, by progressive bodily relaxation procedures while deeply breathing abdominally, by mild hypnosis or by spiritual and religious contemplation.

While the patient is fully relaxed he is asked to imagine mildest social situation that produces little anxiety such as talking to much younger people or to adults who are much less than him in status. When he repeats these scenes again and again in his imagination in this state of relaxation he would gradually overcome any anxiety in dealing with such a situation. When this step is mastered, the therapist will gradually take him to higher levels of anxiety provoking situations such as discussing issues with a polite submissive colleague. The process is gradually repeated until the patient can imagine the highest item in the hierarchy; that of imagining himself giving public talks in front of a critical crowd. It is quite surprising to see that such patients will easily transfer these imagined situations to real life experiences.

I once helped such a socially phobic Saudi young man without being with him all the time. He was the most educated citizen in his village and was elected to be chairman of the village club. They wanted him to give weekly talks. I could not accompany him to his village so I helped him to prepare a hierarchy of gradually more demanding social situations and trained him in progressive muscular relaxation combined with deep breathing and contemplation. I then instructed him to drive his car out of town, relax and imagine himself going through these hierarchical steps by himself. I also instructed him to take a recorder with him and imagine himself giving a public talk in the village and then to listen to his recorded talk in order to listen to himself and to see how he can modify his speech in a way that would be more daring and aggressive. This brilliant young man had to carry out this therapy by himself. In two months he was able to give public talks in the social club of his village without having any hesitance or anxiety. What helped him was his ability to feel his relationship with Allah while going through the imagined scenes and applying these imagined scenes in real life situations. I feel that if you find a Muslim behavior therapist you will definitely get over this treatable problem.

An irresponsible wife who messed up the life of her husband

Question from a Brother

I submitted my problem to you yesterday but I was asked to re-submit it to you today. Unfortunately, I am writing about a matter which I never thought I would ever do in my life. Several years ago, I married a convert to Islam against the wishes of my parents. Because of this reason, we do not stay in the same region. Now, for the last two years we only lived together for a few weeks but we communicate everyday by phone. Three weeks ago, we had an argument after which I did not call her for two weeks. I felt may be she wanted to be left alone. When I called her after that, she told me that she thought I had deserted her. She accordingly gave up all hope in Islam and in us. As a result, she reverted to her old behavior. She had sex with other men and started drinking and dressing immodestly. She is now considering whether she still wishes to remain Muslim and whether we can live together.

I am so much in pain about what has happened. I have never felt so lonely and shattered and destroyed and betrayed. Each day I feel that my life should come to an end to alleviate the pain. My trust in her and anything she says is completely broken. I have read many articles which talk about the punishment for such actions but no one ever writes about what the "victim" should do in these instances. I should mention that we have no children or other dependents and we live in different countries. What do you advise me to do as a Muslim

with respect to my relationship with her?

Answer

Thanks for accepting to reschedule my answer to you but I want you to accept whatever I tell you with a kinship spirit of an uncle talking harshly to his nephew. It is true that I am a counselor and a psychotherapist and it is true that modern counseling has overstressed the "unconditional acceptance" and the "nonjudgmental" attitude to those who come for therapy but I should like to tell you that I also observe my duty as a Muslim who grew up in an Afro-Arab culture. The whole story of your marriage seems to be abnormal from the very beginning. I think you fell in love with this undeserving woman and that your love has blinded you from seeing reality as it really is.

First, you married against the will of your parents and this is Islamically wrong or at least an action that is frowned upon. Our Islamic history tells us that Abdullahi ibn Umar Ibn Khattab married a very beautiful lady whom he loved very much. His father Umar could see that this young wife was causing his son to be less committed to his Islamic tasks. He solemnly told him to divorce her. It was very difficult for Abdullahi to do so. He asked the Prophet (ṣ) about what to do, hoping that he might ask Umar to change his mind. But the Prophet (ṣ) told him if Umar told you to divorce her then you should do so. He did.

So your marriage to that woman without the blessing of your parents was your first mistake. In our cultures, parents will generally change their minds if their children keep repeating their request by using the right tactics. Your second mistake was to allow a newly converted wife to live in her own un-Islamic country without moral or religious support and to see her for a few weeks in two years. If this woman converted to Islam in order to marry you then you should have lived together so that you can help her through the difficult ethical and spiritual transition of conversion. You did not do that. On top of all this, you severed the close bond that you shared with her that might have been given her some strength to continue as a Muslim. You could have maintained this easily through daily phone calls and emails.

However, without being unjust to her, I feel that for a normal wife to indulge in fornication and alcohol intake just because her husband stopped calling her by phone for two weeks after an argument is too incredible to believe. I honestly believe that she was probably secretly engaged in this immoral behavior during the two years of your distant marriage. Less than two weeks is too short for a woman who had been faithful to her husband to develop a new relationship and have an extra marital affair with a man.

Your third calamity is that you seemed to have lost much of your ability to be jealous. How can you be in pain and lonely and wishing to die because you are no longer in contact with such a woman? In your Islamic culture if a wife shows interest or write a love letter to another man, her husband will immediately divorce her in anger. Some may harm her physically. Of course I do not subscribe to such violent actions but it gives me pain to see a young Muslim young man losing his blessed emotion of being jealous and protective to his wife. Even male animals fight against each other ferociously resulting in serious injuries or death over a female. In Islamic *Shariah* a man who accepts to live with a woman who commits adultery is known in Arabic as a *dayyūth*. In an authenticated hadith the Prophet (ṣ) said "No *dayyūth* will be allowed to enter Paradise".

In this entire episode, my dear son, you have only been

motivated by your selfish love and interest. You did not care for your parents nor did you care for your expected children. Where will your future children from this woman live? And is she the good Muslim mother who can bring them up? I think my son you should have an inner reflection on your problem and make an effort to change. You should thank Allah that the character of this woman has now been exposed to you before having children with her. Don't think that your broken heart will continue for long. There is no falling in passionate love that is not followed sooner or later with falling out of it. If it continues it will be a more mature kind of relationship. So be patient for the following months and you will get over your emotional upheaval.

It is obvious to me my son that you are going through a stressful period of your life. A number of studies have shown that divorce and separation are among the most stressful experiences to people all over the world. However, it was found that the passage of time can heal such psychological wounds particularly if the person finds a good friend to console him. A change of environment will also be beneficial. In your case as a Muslim, on top of the help that friendships and change of environment can provide, you have something greater than all of these remedies. Seeking refuge in Allah and struggling for spiritual regeneration can work wonders in changing your psychological condition. Make *du'ā'* to Allah with most sincerity and I am sure He will help you since Allah promises in the Qur'an: "He responds to the call of the one experiencing tremendous need when he calls".

Finally I advise you to look for a devoted, sincere and knowledgeable Muslim Sheikh in your area, who can listen to your problems and comfort you with spiritual counseling that washes away your agony. Try to spend time with him and if you can, try to pray with him and emulate his devotion by taking him as a spiritual guide and a role model. But if you feel that you are going through serious depression, then you must seek professional psychiatric help.

Having said that, I advise you to be firm and frankly tell your wife that your marriage is over but you want her to be a friend. Continue to support her to be a *Muslimah* and send her money or presents. It is possible that she will soon find a more suitable husband because if you live together again, you will definitely be haunted with suspicion of her betraying you with other men. Let her know that her faith in Allah and His apostle is much more important than any un-Islamic behavior that she has committed. A woman who throws away her *hijab*, drinks alcohol, and has friends from the opposite gender but still keeps her faith in Allah is better than a woman who abstains from such immoral acts but loses her faith. So she should be encouraged to keep her faith in Islam and not to give up on God's forgiveness.

Question 40
Lack of concentration in study

Question from Fazila

I am a student. My problem is that I cannot concentrate on my studies and accordingly get poor grades in my exams. Whenever I sit down to study, my mind wanders away to different things. When I come back to the subject of my study and discover my lack of concentration, I become very angry at myself and stop studying. I tried much to improve my concentration but always failed. Can you please help me?

Answer

Your question about lack of concentration is like a question to a physician by a patient who inquires about the reason of having fever or a headache. Such physical disorders may be caused by a host of different causes such as the flu, malaria, tuberculosis or a number of other diseases. Similarly lack of concentration can be caused by many different psychological, educational and biological reasons. Sometimes it is caused by the frustration resulting from a low level of intelligence. A person, who has a low IQ, would find school or university work to be too difficult to understand. They would feel discouraged and bored and whenever they open a book to read, their mind wanders around concentrating on other more interesting activities. Another reason for the lack of concentration is stress and psychological problems at home or at school. For example, a young person whose parents are continuously quarreling, find it difficult to concentrate on their studies at home. At other times, though the student may have good and loving parents who motivate her, she may have her own personal problems with her friends and classmates that continuously distract her attention. Moreover, there are a number of cases where lack of concentration may be caused by some organic factors like deficiency of certain vitamins or abnormal functioning of their hormonal system.

In spite of my lack of information about the causes in your case, I would advise you not to force yourself to sit for long hours of study. For example, if you are to study for four hours then it is better to distribute the time to eight half-hour periods between which you take a break of 10 to 15 minutes doing an interesting activity. Whenever you feel that you are tired and unable to concentrate, do not force yourself to continue and take a short break. Educational psychologists have found that these distributed periods of studying can bring much better results than massed study even though the time used in both cases is the same. Also it may be advisable for you not to study alone. Find a good friend in your class and study with her. Each one of you can read part of the assignment and explain it to each other. If you follow these suggestions you will gradually find your span of attention increasing and your interest in your school work improving. Try to improve your diet particularly with vitamins, minerals, and proteins. Also, regular exercise may be helpful to you giving your body a balanced secretion of necessary hormones and imbue you with health and vitality. Finally, do not forget to continue your *du'ā's* to Allah to ease your academic and social problems.

Question 41

Is marijuana non-addictive and safe to take?

Question from a Brother

The problem I am facing has not yet been properly addressed by a *mufti*. But I need counselling or rehabilitation to help me to get over my problem of substance abuse. I have been taking marijuana. It used to make me feel good and creative. I have a craving to taking it again. Many people take more dangerous drugs like cocaine and heroin. May be marijuana is a lesser evil because it is not addictive and even doctors prescribe it to some patients. When I take it I can contemplate deeply and I feel spiritual and connected with Allah. But I wish if I can get a therapy that saves me from this craving to return to it. I just don't know if whether I am fooling myself and falling into a trap. What are the suggestions that you can give to me to stop thinking about relapsing. I tried many things but failed. Life is monotonous and boring without taking this substance. I failed to find something that fills my emotions and thinking. What are some suggestions can you give me to get rid of this habitual substance abuse? I don't feel like going to a therapist.

Answer

In your statement you were wondering whether you were fooling yourself or as you said "falling in a trap". I must be frank with you in telling you that indeed you have been fooling yourself by rationalizing the intake of marijuana. You have entrapped yourself in this quagmire as a means of escape from the harsh realities of life. First you should know that marijuana is not a safe drug as some pseudo scientists claim. It is addictive. Its long term use was found to cause permanent harmful changes in the brain. It can affect memory and cognitive functions and reduce the level of intelligence. The fact that it is at times given to patients does not mean that it is not addictive. Cancer patients in severe pain are given opium which is one of the most dangerous drugs. Quite often, some medical authorities tell us that certain drugs or tranquilizers are safe and non-addictive but as people engage in using or abusing them, they turn out to be addicting. As early as the late nineteenth century, the famous psychiatrist Sigmund Freud, the founder of psychoanalysis, encouraged people to take cocaine. After using it to help himself with some nasal problems, he claimed that it gave him a better psychological insight and creativity. He pointed that it is not harmful nor is it addictive. As it happened, a number of his creative insights under the influence of cocaine have resulted in his bizarre sexual theories that brought down his psychoanalytic edifice. These theories were formulated after he became addicted to cocaine.

Now scientists tell us that cocaine is a harmful and addictive drug. At one time, scientists told us that smoking is only habitual and not addictive. Now they have changed their mind and we are told that nicotine is addictive and can cause cancer. The same claim of being harmless was said about a leaf that is chewed in Yemen and Ethiopia called "Gat" which has a stimulating component similar to amphetamine. However, further research has shown that though initially it gives its users a feeling of wellbeing and concentration it can eventually be psychologically harmful on those who habitually take it. When the valium tranquilizer was first introduced, we were told that it was not addictive. Anxious people passionately took it in excess. It turned out to be seriously addictive. Now we were told that marijuana may not be addictive or that it may have a number of benefits but recent researches on animals and humans clearly show the opposite.

You are young and being addicted to marijuana at this age can have more serious effects on you in the long run. To get over any addictive substance or habit the person needs to be motivated or forced. Many young Muslim men solemnly take an oath to stop taking the drug and fight any urge to come back to it. This can be helpful very much if the person finds a group of friends who can support him and give him and keep his company so that he can conquer his withdrawal symptoms and his craving. The experience of the black Muslims in the US during the life of Malcolm X was quite encouraging in helping new Muslims get over their addiction to the most harmful drugs such as heroine. This great achievement was accomplished by the fraternal bond and friendship of the members who volunteered to stay with the addict, preventing him from relapsing and encouraging him to bear the ugly withdrawal symptoms until his body is detoxified. After that, they would give him good and healthy food and immediately enlist him in the group of recruits who would help other addicts.

Therefore I advise you to stop procrastinating and to seek the company of a group of good Muslim brothers who can fill your time with spiritually elevating experiences and offer you other kinds of pleasures that would consolidate your efforts in breaking the habit permanently. Also, it may be helpful to you, if you can afford it, to radically change the environment you are living in now. In a study on Sudanese alcoholics that I carried out in the seventies, I found out that the majority of those who took jobs in

Saudi Arabia were completely cured from their alcohol dependence. The time to make this drastic change was the few hours of flight that took them from Khartoum to one of the cities or villages of Saudi Arabia. The highest number of those who cured themselves of alcohol dependence was those who lived in rural and remote areas in Saudi Arabia. Most of those who were cured did not relapse even after coming back to Sudan. Hence, a drastic change of environment and association with committed Muslims can help you overcome your drug dependence.

I also found that many Sudanese drug and alcohol dependents who join a Sufi sect (*tariqah*) by taking an oath from a devoted Sheikh will quickly keep to their new spiritual way of life and totally abandon drugs without any crave. May be you need to find such a spiritually gifted guru.

How to treat an emotionally immature wife?

Question from a Brother

My problem is that my wife hates my parents and speaks to me about them in their absence in the most disrespectful manner. So my parents don't know how much she hates them. I get very angry and sometimes I shout at her. She only cries but does not apologize. Most of her hatred goes to my mother because, as she says, she doesn't give her as much love as the love she gives to my sisters. Whenever I buy something to my parents, she gets very angry. This causes me to shout at her and then she cries. Sheikh, I went to Makkah and made *du'ā'* to Allah to change her heart towards my parents. We got married just two months ago and I get very upset when I think that I will spend the rest of my life with this problem. I thought of divorcing her but she is now pregnant. Sheikh, please tell me what to do.

Answer

What you are saying is not an uncommon problem among young wives and their mothers in law. In some cultures in the Arab world this problem is much more acute than in other African and Asian countries. It is true that there is a hadith of the Prophet Muhammed (ṣ) in which he rebukes the one who favors his wife over his mother and favors his friends over his father. However, you must try to understand the emotional problem of your young wife. It is possible that early in the marriage you said some things about parental obedience that made her feel neglected in terms of love and respect towards her.

It also seems to me that your wife is a dependent person who may suffer from pathological jealousy towards those who share your love. In a case similar to yours, one brother succeeded in solving this problem by telling the mother that his wife speaks highly about her and loves her and he tells the wife the same thing. This kind of diplomacy of white lies is permissible based on a hadith of the Prophet (ṣ). I am not sure whether changing your own behavior towards the wife may help her in regaining her self-confidence and resolving her suppressed animosity towards your parents and especially your mother. The repeated pattern of losing your temper and shouting at her which results in her crying must stop since it has proven to be ineffective in changing her behavior. May be you should try using other tactics such as refusing to talk to her or refusing to share her bed or on the other hand giving her more love and saying things that can raise her morale.

It is obvious that your wife is emotionally immature. I can infer this from her comparison of the amount of love your mother gives to your sisters and that which is given to her. No mature person will expect a woman to love her daughter-in-law the way she loves her own children. I wonder whether your wife's parents are alive and living in your region. I am saying this because in many cases the interference of the mother in changing the negative feelings of her daughter can be of help if the mother herself is a wise mature woman. If her parents are not around or if they cannot be of help then look for some elderly relative whom your wife respects and let him or her advise her in the best possible manner.

My dear son, it seems to me that you and your wife are still young and have little experience in life. You said that you married her just two months ago and that she is now pregnant, so she must have conceived during early weeks of your marriage. Many women during these early weeks of pregnancy may show behavior that is similar to neurotic patients. This is due to the hormonal changes that take place during the early period of pregnancy. The resulting emotional changes can be more acute in young dependent women. They can become quite anxious and depressed. This disorder may also be repeated after birth when the body begins to return to its previous pre-pregnancy state. Furthermore, some women suffer from anxiety, mood disturbance, despair and lack of confidence before having their menstrual period. In a few, this premenstrual disorder can be very severe. It is termed "premenstrual dysphoric disorder". They may act like seriously disturbed patients.

Many inexperienced young men, who observe their pregnant wives feeling sick every morning and becoming irritable and aggressive and refusing their sexual advances, begin to wonder whether they have chosen the right wife. Some husbands may even decide to divorce their wives. I wonder whether your wife is undergoing one of these disorders and that you are overreacting to her temporary psychophysiological reaction.

Finally, I must say that I am impressed by your belief in Allah, who controls his slaves and who can change them as He wishes. Supplication in Makkah will eventually save you from this dilemma. Perform the decision-making prayer and give your wife more love and affection and introduce her to committed Muslim women who can be role models for her.

Question 43

An unusual case of a respected man who needed advice but wrongly treated as psychologically disordered

Question from Aburrahman,
a psychology graduate

Dr. Badri, you have a long experience in counseling and psychotherapy. I wish you can tell me about some of the strangest cases that you have treated.

Answer:

Thanks for your question. I have had many unusual cases during my last 50 years of psychotherapy. I can tell you about only one of them. I was the senior clinical psychologist in one large psychiatric clinic in an African country. The case was that of a distinguished high-ranking officer in the government of that country. He was also known as a good respectable Muslim in his community. He came to the clinic to complain from sudden severe anxiety, insomnia or lack of sleep, intense feelings of guilt and unexplained fear of a future calamity. The psychiatrists in the clinic gave him special attention because of his status but they tried every physical and psychological therapy without success. In such cases, they used to transfer such patients to me in the cognitive behavior therapy unit. I helped the patient to relax physically and mentally using an Islamic contemplative approach that I had designed. He opened up and spoke about his problem for the first time. It was both quite serious and embarrassing.

He finally opened up. As a nine-year-old, he lived with his family in a little town near the frontiers of his country with another state. They chose to live there to be near to his uncle who had to live in that locality because he was a police officer guarding the borders from illegal migrants and smugglers. His uncle was a good pious man who used to help his poor family. He married a woman from another country but for years they did not have any children. The uncle was probably infertile.

The job of his uncle made it necessary for him to periodically leave his house to spend days and nights patrolling the borders. Every time his uncle was away from home, the patient would be asked to sleep in his uncle's house to give company to his uncle's childless wife. This continued for a few years during which he matured into puberty. The childless wife, afraid of being divorced as barren, seduced the patient into having sexual intercourse with her. In a short time, she declared to her husband that she got pregnant. The husband in great joy commemorated the occasion by throwing a big party. His wife gave birth to a baby boy who resembled the patient as if he got him by cloning. He was sure it was his own son and the wife knew it as well but the whole episode was kept a guarded secret and the extreme resemblance in features between the son and his true father was explained away as being an influence of an early common grandfather.

Thereafter, the patient, excelling in his studies, joined the university in the capital city. His family moved there after the death of the uncle. Our patient got married as soon as he secured his university degree and soon became a father to a beautiful baby girl. As the years passed, he got promoted to a very senior government job and his good character and piousness earned him the respect of his citizens.

Out of nowhere, the boy he illegally fathered from his uncle's wife came to visit him in his house. He was a living copy of him. He was happy to see him. He lived with them for some time and fell in love with the patient's daughter. Though younger than him, but she reciprocated his love. He asked her hand! Both his wife and daughter were extremely happy but our patient looked at it as a catastrophe of a young man marrying his own sister! He refused the proposal adamantly but could give no reason for that. Both his wife and daughter were very sad and angry at him. The wife scolded him and accused him of ingratitude to an uncle who was generous to him and his family until his death. "Tell us, what is wrong with the young man", she repeated and he could not utter any convincing answer. Gradually he developed much anxiety and guilt. He reported that he was quite afraid of death, not because he feared death but because he felt that if he suddenly dies in a car crash or heart failure, the boy would marry his sister. He cannot divulge the true reason for his refusal. It will destroy his reputation and devastate the young man and his mother. What advise can you give to this man Aburrahman? Stop reading for a while and think about what to say to him since you are a psychologist and then read what I said in the following paragraph.

I suggested to him to invite his angry wife for a dinner in a good restaurant to gently discuss the issue. Expose the whole story to her. Tell her that this bad wife seduced him into fornication and he could not resist her temptation in his young age. Tell her that the uncle was barren and had no other children.

Tell her to forgive you and to realize why you refused the marriage since you have no doubt that it was your own son who became a 'carbon copy' of you. I told him that his wife would understand the situation and when she does, she will know how to convince her daughter to refuse the marriage. He was greatly relieved by this suggestion. When people are in trouble, they cannot think of a way out even if it were obvious. They are like a person lost in a forest.

He did exactly what I proposed. He was astonished to find his wife so understanding and loving and sympathizing with him in his ordeal but of course she poured all her wrath and fury on the woman who shamelessly seduced a child and lied to her kind-hearted husband. His anxiety and his crippling guilt suddenly disappeared. His wife was able to skillfully convince her daughter and the disappointed young man travelled back to his village without knowing why the mother suddenly changed her mind. He will know in the hereafter.

Question 44

Para-psychological phenomena:
Fact or fiction

Question from Abdal Karim,
a Sudanese lecturer in psychology

Are para-psychological phenomena real or are they fraud and simple coincidences as most Western psychologists would say?

Answer:

Since you are already a lecturer in psychology, I will answer you in a simplified but professional manner so the general reader can understand and you can get a fully comprehensive answer. Parapsychology is the scientific study of paranormal events that cannot be explained by physical laws and normal senses. Parapsychological occurrences include events such as telepathy or communication between human minds that do not use any of our five senses, clairvoyance or remote viewing in which the person gets information from inanimate objects like describing an object in another room or a picture in a sealed envelope, precognition, during wakefulness or sleep in which the person can tell about a future event before it happens, psychokinesis or controlling and moving objects with the power of the mind, near death or out of body experiences and similar events. There is abundant evidence to prove the existence of this phenomenon. Great psychologists such as William James and Jung have strongly supported its existence and recent experimental studies have used statistical analyses to confirm that its occurrence cannot be explained by chance or mere coincidences. However, for reasons I shall mention later, the majority of Western psychologists and scientists refuse, at times irrationally, to believe in its existence.

However, we must acknowledge that the problem with genuine parapsychological phenomena is that they are often confused with other unusual events created by jugglers or magicians or those imposters who use fraudulent ways to claim their abilities in being real psychics. Additionally, authentic parapsychological occurrences can be confused with miracles of Prophets and paranormal episodes of saints and great worshippers "*karamat*". Furthermore, we must know that we are not living alone in this planet. Paranormal phenomena can also be caused by other spiritual beings. Authenticated recent experiences of poltergeists cannot be denied or overlooked or explained away as cheating or psychopathological behavior.

Though Western sources wish to repress such paranormal events, a number of them fail to be denied because of their worldwide validation or their undeniable occurrence. For example the predictive dream of President Abraham Lincoln that accurately foretold his assassination and where in the White House his body, guarded and shrouded by the American flag, will be placed. Another such dream came from the famous German physiologist, Otto Loewi who won the Nobel Prize in 1938 for his work on the chemical transmission of nerve impulses. He thought of the idea but failed to prove it. He gave up on it but after 17 years he saw a dream that instructed him on how to prove his assumption experimentally. He got up from his sleep, rushed to his laboratory and followed the instructions in his dream by applying it on the heart of a frog. It proved his chemical transmission and earned him the Nobel Prize.

An example of an unexplained phenomenon that cannot be refused is Foreign Language Syndrome. It certainly exists and cannot be fully explained. After a serious accident or injury to the brain, a person, after momentarily losing consciousness, finds himself talking in a foreign language that he had not been able to speak before the accident. One woman, who never left her small city in the US, found herself after the accident speaking Russian. She did not know it was Russian until a person who spoke the language told her it was so. By inventing a psychological term such as "Foreign Language Syndrome", for a paranormal phenomenon, Western psychiatrists think that they have solved the problem. It is just like a person who attaches a handle and a tag to a locked suitcase without a key. By fixing the handle and giving it a name he cannot know what is inside the suitcase! His belief that he has solved the problem is a mere illusion!

If there is such a strong scientific and highly respected anecdotal confirmation for paranormal phenomena why is it that there is such an intense resistance to its validation from the secular scientific community to the extent that unbiased researchers consider their attitude to be a conspiracy against the paranormal? Historically, the Western world erected its scientific and technological revolution on the ruins of the Church of the Middle Ages and its brutal retribution against scientists and free thinkers. As an overreaction against the Church, Western scientists developed an opposite extreme position against religion and its unseen beliefs. This extreme behavior was described by some cynical thinkers as a colossal posttraumatic reaction!

The scientific method that helped them to establish themselves as the world superpower eventually became the only acid test for differentiating between truth and falsity. So, any event that cannot be confirmed by the senses and validated by its repetition under the same conditions cannot be verified. That is why paranormal events create this conscious and unconscious denial and animosity. For secular scientists to accept that gifted persons can tell the future or communicate beyond the senses or float outside their terminally sick bodies to see what doctors are doing with it would bring down their entire materialistic scientific edifice. Such events may confirm the existence of a human soul and point to the possibility of life after death. So they strongly cling to their singular epistemological position that refuses to accept any other way of knowing like intuition. Their thought is based on a worldview of secularism that has its staunch beliefs about the nature of man as an animal without a soul. It is as I once said, "a religion of irreligiousness".

I wish to state here that scientific rigor alone is not really the deciding factor in accepting or rejecting a branch of knowledge like parapsychology as secular psychologists wish us to believe. Western psychology is happy to entertain unscientific and at times absurd theories and practices if they support or do not challenge their secular and humanistic worldview. Freudian psychoanalysis is a good example for that. With all the recent collected evidences about the unscientific and fraudulent claims of Freud, his theories and practices continue to litter the textbooks and journals of psychology.

Furthermore, it is really unfair to strictly apply the most rigorous empirical conditions on genuine anecdotal parapsychological occurrences. They are by their very nature unpredictable. If one clearly sees a dream in which he predicted future events and they happen in a way that is statistically significant beyond any doubt, we cannot apply the narrow scientific criterion of repeatability to verify this claim. We can't tell him to go to sleep and repeat a similar predictive dream! In a similar manner, many cases of telepathy and clairvoyance cannot be repeatable.

As Muslims, we believe that all humans have a dual nature of matter and a holy spirit breathed into our clay by Allah. It is this spiritual component that can go beyond time and space to give us a glimpse of the unseen. We believe in the miracles of Prophets that are much greater and different from any paranormal occurrences or witchcraft or actions of jinn. This differentiation is clearly shown to us in the Qur'anic story of the contest between Prophet Musa or Moses (ṣ) and the magicians who were using witchcraft. It was an encounter between the paranormal abilities of witchcraft and that of the miraculous support of God. The stick of Musa miraculously swallowed their sticks and ropes. It was this incident that clearly shows that though miracles and paranormal events superficially look like each other, miracles can easily invalidate and supersede all forms of the paranormal.

We also believe that sincere worshippers can be bestowed with paranormal support. In this respect, the famous authenticated telepathic episode of Umar Ibn Khattab the second successor or *khalifah* of Prophet Muhammad (ṣ) is a good example. This case was witnessed and heard by hundreds of congregants in the Prophet's mosque in Madinah. Umar was giving his Friday sermon but he suddenly shouted words that were totally unrelated to his sermon. He shouted at the top of his voice to the commander of the Muslim army fighting the Persian army thousands of kilometers away from Madinah. He yelled to him to take refuge in the mountain. The Muslim congregation asked him after the prayers why he shouted with these incoherent words. He said I suddenly felt that the Muslim army was about to be attacked from behind by Persian fighters. He said, "The only way to obstruct their shrewd plan is for the Muslim army to take refuge in a mountain in the area of the battlefield". After the long journey back to Madinah, Saria, the commander of the Muslim army arrived to tell everybody that he heard the voice of Umar and followed his advice and won the battle.

Selected bibliography

Works in English

Badri, M. B. *Contemplation: An Islamic Psychospiritual Study*. London: International Institute of Islamic Thought, 2000.

Badri, M. B. "Counseling and psychotherapy from an Islamic perspective." *Al-Shajarah: Journal of the International Institute of Islamic Thought and Civilization*, vol.1, nos. 1 & 2 (1996).

Badri, M. B. *Islam and Alcoholism*. Washington: American Trust Publications, 1976.

Badri, M. B. *The AIDS Crisis: A Natural Product of Modernity's Sexual Revolution*. Kuala Lumpur: Medeena Books, 2000.

Badri, M. B. *The Dilemma of Muslim Psychologists*. London: MWH Publishers, 1979.

Beck, A. *Cognitive Therapy and the Emotional Disorders*. New York: New American Library, 1976.

Benson, Herbert. *Timeless Healing*. London: Simon & Schuster, 1988.

Brown, S. C., ed. *Philosophy of Psychology*, Royal Institute of Philosophy. London: The Macmillan Press Ltd., 1974.

Dols, M. W. *Majnun: The Madman in Medieval Islamic Society*, Oxford: Clarendon Press, 1992.

Kiev, A. *Magic, Faith and Healing.* London: Free Press, 1964.

Peck, M. S. *Glimpses of the Devil: A Psychiatrist's Personal Account of Possession, Exorcism and Redemption.* New York: Simon & Schuster, 2005.

Peck, M. S. *The Road Less Travelled: A new Psychology of Love, Traditional Values and Spiritual Growth.* London: Arrow Books, 1990.

Wolpe, J. *Psychotherapy by Reciprocal Inhibition.* Stanford: Stanford University Press, 1958.

Works in Arabic

Badri, M. B. Modern Psychotherapy from an Islamic Perspective. In *Conference on the Islamization of the Behavioural Sciences* (Proceedings). Washington: International Institute of Islamic Thought, 1987.

Al-Irgisoosi, M. K. *The Influence of Muscular Relaxation and Islamic Prayer (Ruqya) in the Treatment of Essential Hypertension.* Unpublished doctoral thesis, University of Khartoum, Sudan, 1992.

al-Ghazali, Abu Hamid. *Ihya' 'Ulum Al-Din* (Revival of the Religious Sciences). Beirut: Dar al-Qalam, n.d.

al-Balkhi, Abu Zaid. *Masalih al-abdan wa al-anfus* (Sustenance for Body and Soul). Frankfurt: Institute for the History of Arabic-Islamic Science, 1984.

Made in the USA
Middletown, DE
25 March 2021